FOLENS HISTORY

G000162362

MEDIEVAL REALMS

RICHARD ALLISON
CAROLE BROWN

Acknowledgements

The authors and publishers would like to thank the following for permission to reproduce photographs and other material:

B T Batsford Limited (6C)
A & C Black (Publishers) Limited (12A)
Blackie & Son Limited (6E)
Bodleian Library, University of Oxford (7A (MS. Douce 6, fol. 22r); 13F(MS. Bodley Rolls 3, last row))
Book Club Associates (12F; 14A)
By permission of The British Library (4E (MS. Add 42130); 5F (MS. Harl 5102, fol. 32); 6B (MS. Roy 14 CVII, fol. 9); 7B (MS. Add 20698, fol. 17); 7D (MS. Eg 1894, fol. 2v); 7H; 12B (MS. Claud B IV, fol. 59); 14B (MS. Add 42130, fol. 147v); 14C (MS. Cott Ch XIX.V); 16C (MS. Roy 18 E I, fol. 165v); 16D (MS. Roy 18 E I, fol 172r); 19B)
Reproduced by courtesy of the Trustees of the British Museum (19A)
CADW: Welsh Historic Monuments. Crown Copyright (13B; 13D)
Cambridge University Press (6D)
Curtis Brown Limited on the behalf of the estate of Arthur Duggan. © A Duggan (5C)
Evans Brothers Limited (1D)
Jeremy Haslam (8C)
Michael Holford Photographs (1G; 2C; 2I; 2K; 3B)
Judges Postcards Limited, Hastings (8A)
Macdonald & Co (Publishers) Limited (14D)
Mansell Collection (5A; 5B; 11A; 17A)
Reproduced by courtesy of the Trustees, The National Gallery, London (19C)
The National Portrait Gallery (16A; 17B; 18A; 18D)
The Scottish National Portrait Gallery. William Hole, 'The Battle of Bannockburn' (detail) (14H)
Spartacus (15J)
© Times Newspapers Limited 1987. The Times, May 22, 1987. Report Mark Ellis, photograph John Rogers (15A)
The Board of Trinity College Dublin (13E)
By courtesy of the Board of Trustees of the Victoria & Albert Museum (4C; 7E)
Wales Tourist Board (13A)
Windsor Castle, Royal Library. ©1990 Her Majesty The Queen (12H)

Illustrators:

Denby Designs
Jillian Luff of Bitmap Graphics
Paul Nicholls

Cover:

Design - Tanglewood Graphics, Broadway House, The Broadway, London SW19
Illustration - Abacus Publicity Limited

First published 1990 by Folens Limited, Albert House, Apex Business Centre, Boscombe Road, Dunstable LU5 4RL, England.

ISBN 1 85276 120 2

Printed in Great Britain by Eagle Colour Books Limited.

CONTENTS

1000
1100
1200
1300
1400
1500
1600
1700
1800
1900
2000

Target

* To recognise bias.
* To consider the viewpoints of opposing sides.

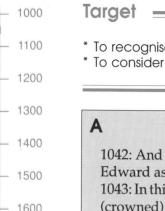

A

1042: And the whole nation then received Edward as king as was his right by birth.
1043: In this year Edward was consecrated (crowned) king in Winchester on Easter Sunday.

Anglo-Saxon Chronicle.

 Using this source suggest two reasons why Edward was invited to be king.
(CLUE TO SUCCESS: Look carefully at the 1042 entry. Try to read between the lines!)

After the Romans left Britain in 410 A.D. all the changes and new ideas which they had brought began to be lost. In the centuries which followed Britain was invaded by the Anglo Saxons and the Vikings. However, for the ordinary person, these invasions changed the way in which they lived very little.

During these centuries, Britain had many kings. Our story begins in 1042 when Edward the Confessor, as he became known, was invited to be king of England.

Harold's Claim

B

1066: And Earl Harold succeeded to the kingdom of England as the king had granted it to him and men had also chosen him.

Anglo-Saxon Chronicle of Peterborough Abbey.

 According to the writer of this source why did Harold become king?

C

1065: Yet did the wise king (Edward) entrust his kingdom to a man of high rank, to Harold himself, the noble earl who ever faithfully obeyed his noble lord (King Edward).

Anglo-Saxon Chronicle. Written 1066.

 What can we learn about Harold and his relationship with King Edward from this source?

Edward the Confessor

Edward, who had lived in Normandy for most of his life, was invited by the Witan (the council of the English chiefs) to come to England as king. Edward is often called the Confessor because he was a very religious person. He married the sister of one of England's most powerful noblemen, Harold, Earl of Godwin. However, Edward and his wife did not have any children, so when he died England was again faced with the problem of who should be king.

The Contenders for the Crown

The two main contenders were Harold Godwinsson, Earl of Wessex and William, Duke of Normandy. You can read about their claims to the throne in this unit. There were two other contenders: Harald Hardrada who claimed that he was king of Norway and Denmark. He argued that as the Danes had conquered England he, as king of Denmark, should be king of England as well. You can read about what happened to Hardrada later in Unit 2. The other was Edgar Atheling, the young, grand nephew of Edward the Confessor. Edgar had been brought up in Hungary, so he had few supporters in England. Although he came to England he was unable to succeed in his claim to the throne.

D

For the last 13 years of his reign Edward left most of the business of governing England to Harold ... Harold governed England well.

A New English History 1. Alan Bullock, 1969.

 How does this source support Harold's claim to the throne?

F

Harold swore an oath to William ... freely and distinctly. Harold promised that he would act as William's representative at the court of his master King Edward and that after Edward's death he would do everything in his power to confirm (help) William to his succession to the throne of England.

William of Poitiers, chronicler to Duke William of Normandy. Written 1066.

 What do you think the words 'freely and distinctly' mean?

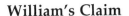
William's Claim

E

Edward, King of the English, loved William of Normandy as much as if the Duke had been his brother ... and he had long before appointed him as his heir. (promised William the English throne) ... In order to confirm his promise by an oath (promise) he sent Harold, the wealthiest of all his subjects to William.

William of Poitiers, chronicler to Duke William of Normandy. Written 1066.

In your own words explain the meaning of this source to a friend.

CORE ACTIVITY

1 Look at each source in turn.
● Write the source letter, say who wrote it and when it was written.
● Say whether or not the source is biased and give reasons. You could use a quotation from the source to support your answer.
● Decide whether Harold or William had the strongest claim to the throne and give reasons for your answer.

Harold swearing an oath in front of William to help him become king of England. From the Bayeux Tapestry, made on Norman orders shortly after the battle. Harold claimed that he was tricked into making the promise.

 What do you think might be in the boxes which Harold is shown touching as he makes his promise?

EXTENSION ACTIVITY

1 Find a friend to work with.
● One of you should take the role of Harold and find out as much as possible about him. The other should take the role of William and find out as much as possible about him.
● Each of you should prepare a list of reasons for your claim to the English throne.
● Invite 2 or 3 other people in the class to your 'court'. They must listen to each of you present your arguments and then decide who they think should have the throne.

2. 1066: BATTLE OF HASTINGS

1000
1100
1200
1300
1400
1500
1600
1700
1800
1900
2000

Target

* To assess the reliability of evidence.
* To make deductions based on the evidence.
* To reconstruct an event from a given viewpoint.

The Bayeux Tapestry begins with King Edward sending Harold to Normandy with a message that the throne is for William. However, Harold is shipwrecked and held by Count Guy de Ponthieu, until William pays a ransom.

Harold then spent some time at the court of William. Whether Harold promised to help William of his own free will or whether William tricked Harold into making the promise we will probably never know. However, we do know that once Harold had been crowned king, William began making preparations for the invasion of England.

You will have noticed that all the Norman sources used in Unit 1 mention that Harold promised to help William gain the English throne. We know that Harold travelled to Normandy in 1064.

A

Duke William took the advice of his supporters and decided to avenge (seek revenge) his insult and lay claim to his inheritance by force of arms... in his great wisdom the Duke had ships constructed and fitted them out with weapons, crews, supplies of food and all things necessary for war.

William of Poitiers, chronicler to Duke William of Normandy. 1066.

 What is the meaning of the words '... lay claim to his inheritance by force of arms'?

B

1066: At that time throughout all England, a portent (a sign) was seen in the heavens. Some declared that the star was a comet, which some call 'the long haired star': it first appeared ... on 24 April and shone every night for a week.

Anglo-Saxon Chronicle.

The comet was thought to be a sign that something bad was about to happen.

 Do you think people at that time were more superstitious than today? Give reasons for your answer.

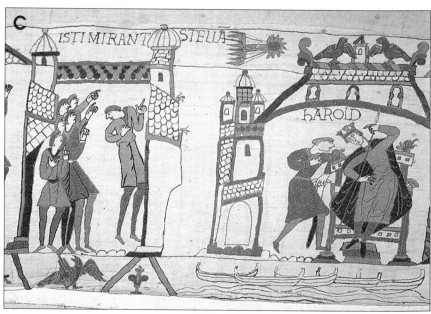

ISTI MIRANT STELLA

HAROLD

A comet is seen.

 *How does this piece of the Bayeux Tapestry support what we are told in **B**?*

The battle at Stamford Bridge

You will remember another contender for the throne of England was Harald Hardrada. On hearing that Harold had become king, he too made preparations for war.

D

> Harald, king of Norway, and earl Tostig and their force had gone from their ships beyond York to Stamford Bridge...Then Harold, king of the English came upon them unawares beyond the bridge. They joined battle and fierce fighting went on until late in the day: and there Harald, king of Norway was slain and earl Tostig and countless numbers of men with them, both English and Norwegians.
>
> *Anglo-Saxon Chronicle. 1066.*

Find another person and explain to them in your own words the story told here.

The Battle of Hastings

The Battle of Stamford Bridge was fought on 25th September, 1066. Shortly after this messengers brought the news to Harold that Duke William of Normandy had landed at Pevensey on the south coast on 28th September. Harold gathered his army together and marched south. The battle took place on October 14th.

F

> Then Duke William sailed from Normandy into Pevensey, on the eve of Michaelmas (28th September). As soon as his men were fit for service, they constructed (built) a castle at Hastings. When King Harold was informed of this, he gathered together a great host (army) and came to oppose him at the grey apple-tree, and William came upon him unexpectedly before his army was set in order.
>
> *Anglo-Saxon Chronicle. 1066.*

E

King Harold
Duke William
King of Norway

The Sites of the Battles of 1066.

How far would Harold's troops have to march before they fought in the Battle of Hastings? (CLUE TO SUCCESS: Use the map scale to help you)

G

> ...braying (blowing) of trumpets announced the outset of battle on both sides. Eager and brave the Normans were first to attack... The English hurled (threw) javelins and missiles of all sorts, dealing savage blows with their axes...Then the knights rode forward ... they bravely engaged the enemy with their swords. The din of the shouting from the Normans on this side, from the barbarians (English) on that, could hardly be heard for the clash of their weapons and the groans of the dying.
>
> *William of Poitiers, chronicler to William. Written c.1066.*

H

The English were helped by the advantage of their high position which, massed tightly together they held without attempting to advance... the weapons which they fought with easily cut through shields and other protective armour... The Norman infantry turned in flight... almost the whole battle line of Duke William fell back, a fact which can be admitted without affront (insult) to the Normans...The Normans imagined that their Duke had fallen, but he rushed after his retreating troops, dragged off his helmet and showed his bared head. 'Look at me!' he shouted, 'I am still alive! With God's help I shall win'... They took new courage from his words and he himself rode on again at their head.

William of Poitiers, chronicler to William. Written c.1066.

 What view does the chronicler seem to have of William?

The English on Senlac Hill.
*Make a list of anything from this which supports what the chronicler says in **H**.*

J

The English who were so sure of themselves fought with all their might, they were so tightly massed that the men who were killed could hardly fall on the ground. The Normans realised that they could never overcome the vast army of their enemies... They therefore withdrew, pretending to turn in flight. Some thousand or more of the English rushed boldly forward; suddenly the Normans turned their horses, cut off the force which was pursuing (chasing) them, encircled them and massacred (killed) them to the last man. Twice the Normans used this trick with equal success.

William of Poitiers, chronicler to William. Written c.1066.

CORE ACTIVITIES

Explain in your own words the successful tactic the Normans used against the English.

1 Historians must always ask themselves 'How do we know about history?'.
- Look back again at all the evidence in this Unit.
- What are the three main sources of information which have been used?
- Do you think the sources that have used are reliable evidence? Explain your answer.

2 Imagine that a friend has said that they do not believe the Battle of Hastings happened.
- How would you prove to them that it did. *(CLUE TO SUCCESS: Think about: where you might take them; what sort of artefacts you might show them)*
- Make a list of all the other evidence you would use.

3 In **F** the person writing the Anglo-Saxon Chronicle says, '... and William came upon him (Harold) unexpectedly before his army was set in order'. This seems to suggest that Harold was not ready to fight. This may be one reason why Harold lost the battle, but there are many other reasons.
- Look back again through all the sources and photographs.
- Try to find reasons for Harold's army not being ready.
- You could write a short article or design a cartoon strip entitled, 'Why I think Harold lost the Battle of Hastings'.
- Show your article to other people and read theirs. Talk about any differences in your articles.

Harold is killed.

 Which figure do you think is Harold?

 What is happening in the border below the battle?

L

The English were weakening and suffered heavy losses...As the daylight began to fade, the English troops realised they no longer had the strength to fight the Normans, their king was dead and his brothers with him; those who remained were exhausted. The English turned in flight and made off at full speed, some on horses they had.

William of Poitiers, chronicler to William. Written c.1066.

 At what time of day does the battle seem to have ended?

EXTENSION ACTIVITY

4 Look back at **K**. For many years it has been believed that Harold died with an arrow in his eye. However, historians now think that Harold might be the man whose legs are being hacked with a sword by a Norman on horseback.

- Decide which figure you think is Harold and support your answer with reasons.
  (CLUES TO SUCCESS: The Latin words 'Harold Rex interfectus est' embroidered above the two figures mean, 'Here King Harold dies')
- Look at all the photographs of the Tapestry.
- How are men shown when they are dead?
- Could both the figures be Harold?
- Give reasons for your answer.

1 Working with other members of your class you are going to design and make your own tapestry of the Battle of Hastings. The real Tapestry showed the Norman view of what happened. You are going to make one which shows the English view.

- Discuss with other members of your group which scenes you are going to include. You may want to leave out some of the scenes shown on the Bayeux Tapestry.
- Think about: Harold's promise; the Battle of Stamford Bridge; how to represent the figures of Harold and William; how to organise yourselves as a group to do all the work.
- Try to find a good place to display your tapestry. It might help if you could see a full copy of the Bayeux Tapestry. Your teacher might have one.

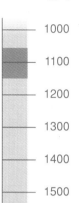

1000
1100
1200
1300
1400
1500
1600
1700
1800
1900
2000

Targets

* To learn about life in Norman England.
* To compare life at this time with our own life today.

In the 100 years after the Battle of Hastings the gap between the Norman rulers and the native English remained very clear. While villagers lived in small huts, the king and his barons owned a string of stone castles which dominated the countryside.

England at this time was still a land of forest, marsh and wild moorland. Around each village were woods and these were used to provide fuel and food, and for hunting small game. Farming was the main occupation for most of the population, though usually villages produced only sufficient food for the lord and the local community. There was little left over for market and in bad years disease often took the lives of the weaker villagers.

The Estate System

William the Conqueror had shared his kingdom with those who had fought alongside him. These barons or 'tenants in chief' helped to control the English. They also provided the king with knights to guard royal castles and fight if war broke out. These knights in turn became tenants of the barons, running each village or manor with its demesne farm, and letting the rest to villeins and cottars (who had little or no land for themselves). Each tenant swore an oath of fealty (loyalty) to his lord. The peasants at the bottom of society had to obey the lord. They could never leave the manor without his permission. Since food could only be grown if the peasants laboured, it was in the lord's interest to keep them working long hours in his fields.

Nowadays the word 'estate' means an area but it can also mean a class in society. In Norman England there were three estates or classes of society: the king and nobles, the Church and the Common People. This system was also called 'feudal', from the Latin word 'feodum' meaning land held by a tenant.

Education

Few people learnt to read and write. Most noblemen preferred to employ a secretary. Small schools were plentiful in towns where clergymen prepared boys for the priesthood. Latin, grammar and dialectic (the art of argument) were the main subjects; a few scholars studied arithmetic, astronomy and music.

A

N

Castles built by 1086

Durham
York
Lincoln
Shrewsbury
Gloucester
London
Winchester
Exeter
Hastings

0   200
kilometres

Norman castles and lands of major barons.

The Norman army foraging for food.

 What information does this scene from the Bayeux Tapestry give us about the countryside at the time?

The ruling class

There were about 150 barons who all spoke French. All legal documents were written in Latin, the language of the Church. Soon rulers and their servants found it helpful to know both English and French. Society was more bilingual in 1150 than it is today.

According to the Domesday Book, written in 1086, 20 towns had a population of over 1 000. Only London had more than 10 000 inhabitants. Despite their size, these towns were important for fairs and markets, where news of the wider world could be heard. Gradually they developed their own councils, based on guilds of merchants and craftsmen.

Communications

The main roads had been built by the Romans. They linked London to the North, West and Wales. They were rarely repaired except near towns, where the local baron charged tolls for using a bridge or setting up a stall in the market square. Traffic was fairly light - pedlars on foot, merchants on horseback and cartloads of hay or wool. However, in 1100 a new bell for Durham Cathedral was brought from London on a wagon drawn by 22 oxen.

CORE ACTIVITY

1 The Estate System was like a social pyramid, with few people in the highest class and most at the bottom.
  ● Draw a diagram to show each of these levels in Norman society.
  ● Remember to label each level.
  ● Choose your own title for the diagram.

EXTENSION ACTIVITIES

1 ● In your notebook divide a page into two columns. At the top of one column write 1150. At the top of the other column write this year's date.
  ● Using the headings below, write about England then and now. You should be able to think of something to put in the second column but if not, look for additional information.
    - population
    - the countryside
    - farming
    - lords and villagers
    - language
    - roads
    - education

2 ● Working with a friend discuss a journey between London and another part of England in 1150.
  ● What could you say about the roads, transport, speed, the countryside and towns?

4. THE MEDIEVAL VILLAGE

Targets

* To find out how people lived in a medieval village.
* To investigate their viewpoints and feelings at that time.

We know that at this time most of the people of England lived in villages and that they earned their living from the land. Village life was dominated by farming.

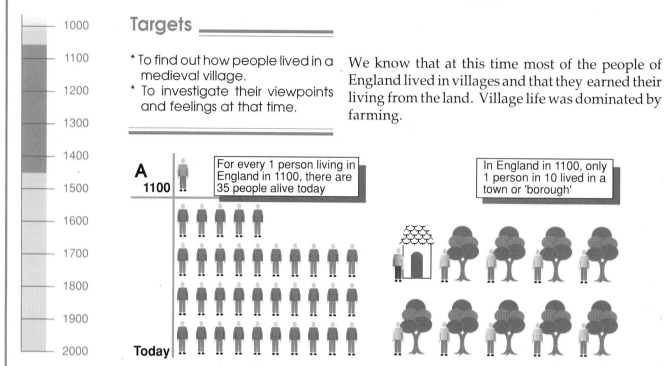

A 1100

For every 1 person living in England in 1100, there are 35 people alive today

Today

In England in 1100, only 1 person in 10 lived in a town or 'borough'

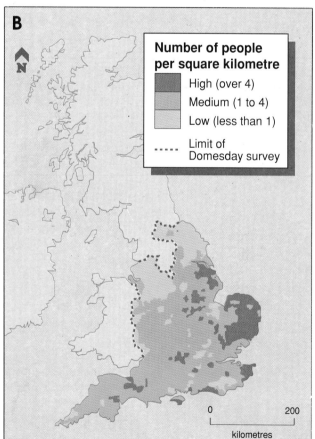

Number of people per square kilometre

High (over 4)
Medium (1 to 4)
Low (less than 1)
----- Limit of Domesday survey

0   200
kilometres

England's population according to the Domesday Book, 1086.
Look at a modern map of England.   Name 3 counties which had a high population in 1066 and 3 which had a low population.

The Domesday Book

Domesday Book is the source for these figures. This was a very detailed survey carried out on William's orders in 1086, showing who owned every piece of land, the number and types of people in each district and the value of their property. Knowing that the probable result of such an investigation was higher taxation it was called 'domesday' like the day of judgment. However, the survey is not complete. Major towns like London and Winchester and parts of the northern counties are omitted.

Villagers at work.

Using the historical evidence let us try to find out how one family lived in a typical medieval village.

Archaeologists have provided us with evidence of the size, shape and contents of a family home in a medieval village, but we have very few documents which tell us about the people themselves.

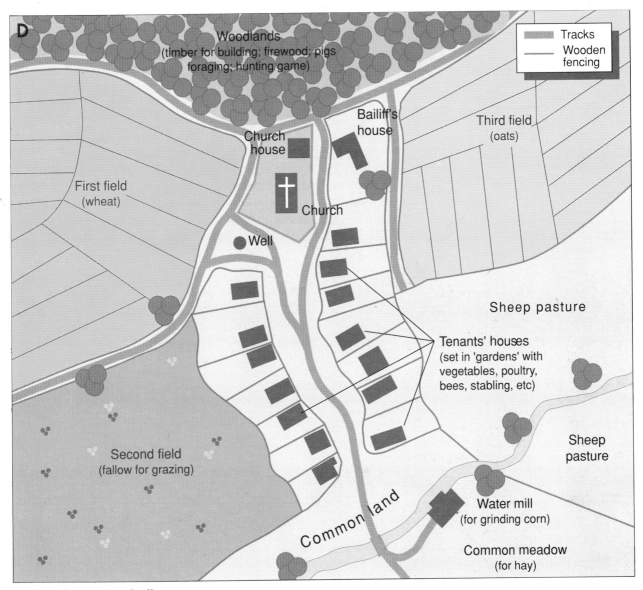

A plan of a medieval village.

 Why do you think there were 3 fields?

 Why were these divided into strips?

In the open fields the main crops were wheat, rye, oats, peas and beans. Livestock included oxen (for pulling ploughs and carts) cattle and sheep, which supplied milk and wool. They also manured the open field after harvesting. Bees were important because honey was the only sweetener.

The life of the village was dominated by farming. Whatever the season, people would work in the fields throughout the hours of daylight. The weather was very important. A drought or a wet summer or a very hard winter could all cause famine in the village.

13

The farming year.

 Which of these tasks would be the most tiring ?

Family Life

A family would probably own one small pig which would be left to forage (search for food) around the village and the woods. On special occasions like Christmas the pig would be killed and some meat salted or smoked to keep for the cold months of the new year. Salt would be one of the few items that villagers would have to buy from a market or pedlar.

Everyday meals consisted of a stew or 'mess' of oatmeal gruel, peas, beans, onions and cabbages which were grown in the garden or 'toft'. The pot might also contain flour dumplings and even nettles, dandelions and ground elder. This would be eaten with coarse black rye bread and washed down with water or ale. Everyone had their own knife but ladles, bowls, mugs and spoons would all be wooden.

Along with the cooking pot, the family's main possession would be an ox. In cold weather all the livestock, including hens, were brought inside to share the meagre warmth. The only light would come from reeds dipped in mutton fat. These were called 'rush lights'.

Here is the view of a medieval writer who wanted rich people to treat villeins with kindness:

F

The poorest folk are our neighbours ... in their hovels, overburdened with children ... whatever they save by spinning they spend on rent, or on milk and oatmeal for food. And they themselves are often famished with hunger and wretched with the miseries of winter - cold, sleepless nights, when they get up to rock the cradle cramped in a corner, and rise before dawn to card and comb the wool, to wash and scrub and mend, and wind yarn and peel rushes for their rushlights ... while the Friars feast on roast venison, they have bread and thin ale, with perhaps a scrap of cold meat or stale fish ... I tell you, it would be a real charity to ... comfort these cottagers along with the blind and the lame.

The Vision of Piers Plowman. William Langland, c.1390.

G

A reconstruction of a medieval cottage.

 What kind of evidence might have been used by the artist for this reconstruction?

Throughout the year feast days, saints' days and other holy days would provide a break from the normal routine. The Church was the centre of village life. It was the largest and most familiar building where you met everyone and really felt part of the community as a member of the congregation. After the service the church would be used for feasting and drinking on a Holy Day. Outside on the green there would be archery, wrestling, singing and dancing.

CORE ACTIVITY

1 Using all the evidence from this unit:
● Write an account of two days in the life of a family from the village. Choose one member of the family and try to give their point of view.
- **Day 1 Working Day**
  Try to mention: what you would wear; all the tasks you would have to do; a conversation during the main meal; which part of the day you enjoyed most and least.
- **Day 2 A Feast Day**
  Explain what happened and which part of the day you enjoyed the most.

1 Look at Core Activity 1.
● Working in a small group organise a short play about the two days.
● Decide which member of the family you will be.
● What were the main events which you should include?
● Try to put together three or four scenes about each of these incidents.

5. HENRY II AND THOMAS BECKET

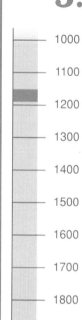

1000
1100
1200
1300
1400
1500
1600
1700
1800
1900
2000

Targets

* To understand the importance of individuals in causing events.
* To identify long and short term causes and results.

In twelfth century England everyone believed in Christianity. The Church, ruled by the pope in Rome, was very powerful. The king wanted to control all his people, yet priests, monks and nuns had to obey the pope rather than the king.

The Pope claimed to be able to ex-communicate (cut off) a king from the Church. His subjects were then free to disobey him.

The Church had its own laws and courts which tried the clergy. Punishments were mild compared to royal courts. Anyone who could read and write could claim to be a cleric.

Bishops and abbots owned large estates and some lived in great luxury. Everyone paid a tithe (a tenth part) of their income to the Church.

V

The King appointed his friends to be bishops and royal advisers.

The King had a duty to enforce the law. His judges and juries dealt severely with all crimes. For example, thieves could be whipped, have a hand cut off or be hanged.

The King knew that bishops would not use their wealth to raise armies to challenge him.

 Which 'team' do you think is the best? Why?

St. Thomas Becket.

The penance of Henry II.

Given the importance of the Church no one was surprised when in 1162 King Henry II arranged for his close friend and adviser, Thomas Becket, to be Archbishop of Canterbury.

The conflict

Henry and Thomas had been great friends. They worked hard and also enjoyed hunting, joking and exploring the night life of London together. When he became archbishop, Thomas seemed to change completely. He protected the rights of the Church and refused to allow the king to punish clergy in the royal courts. When Henry tried to arrest him Thomas fled abroad. Six years later he was allowed to return but his attitudes had not changed. In an angry mood, Henry asked 'Who will deliver me from this low born priest?' Four knights replied by hacking Thomas to death in his cathedral.

The king admitted his guilt and was publicly flogged by the monks of Canterbury. In 1173 Thomas was made a saint.

C

He was immensely tall ... very thin ... he was dark, with black hair and a great beak of a Norman nose ... he was a good judge of wine ... and a keen sighted hunter and horseman.

A description of Becket from, Thomas Becket of Canterbury. A. Duggan, 1967.

 What are the differences between the descriptions in **C** and **D**?

D

He had a red, freckled face, a large round head ... a fiery look and a harsh cracked voice ... His frame was stocky with a pronounced tendency to corpulence (fatness) ... which he tempered (controlled) by exercise ... he did not allow a moment's rest. Beyond doubt was his keenness for hunting.

A description written soon after Henry's death by a monk, Gerald of Wales.

CORE ACTIVITY

1 Look at the evidence generally.
  ● Why did the 'quarrel' take place?
  ● What was the result - did Henry or Thomas win or was it a draw? *(CLUE TO SUCCESS:*Think about both the short term and long term results)
  ● How far did the character and attitudes of the two main individuals involved affect the result?
  ● What details are confirmed by **F**? It was drawn by a monk soon after the event.
  ● Does it provide any additional information ?

E

▼ Henry won because he still chose the bishops and abbots.

▼ The church won because clergy were still tried in its own courts. These also dealt with ordinary people's disputes over wills and marriage contracts.

▼ Henry's humiliation destroyed the people's support for the monarchy. Its weakness gave the barons the opportunity to bring terror and plunder to the land. In 1215 they forced Henry's son, King John, to sign Magna Carta, granting them enormous privileges as well as freedom to the Church.

Henry and Thomas: three modern views of who had won.

The murder of Thomas Becket.

EXTENSION ACTIVITY

1 ● Using all the evidence you can find, write a news programme about this event. You could include:
    - the background to the murder
    - the murder itself
    - a few comments by an 'on the spot' reporter about what is likely to happen next
Make it dramatic! You could work in a group to prepare the script and record it as a radio programme.

Targets

* To understand that one event can have a variety of causes and results.

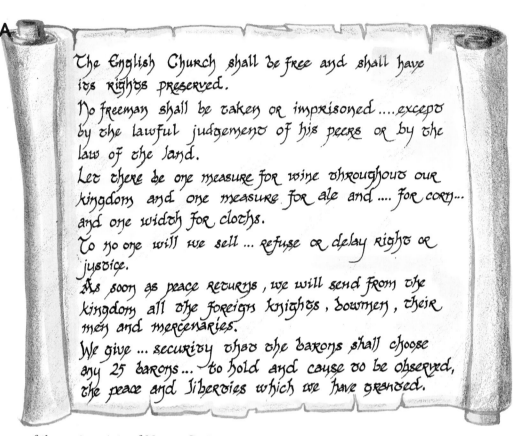

The English Church shall be free and shall have its rights preserved.

No freeman shall be taken or imprisoned .....except by the lawful judgement of his peers or by the law of the land.

Let there be one measure for wine throughout our kingdom and one measure for ale and .... for corn... and one width for cloths.

To no one will we sell ... refuse or delay right or justice.

As soon as peace returns, we will send from the kingdom all the foreign knights, bowmen, their men and mercenaries.

We give ... security that the barons shall choose any 25 barons ... to hold and cause to be observed, the peace and liberties which we have granted.

Some of the main points of Magna Carta.

On the morning of June 15th 1215 King John signed the Great Charter (Magna Carta) in a river meadow at Runnymede, near Windsor. A memorial marking the spot commemorates this document as the 'symbol of freedom under law'.

Faced with a civil war against 40 of his barons, John was persuaded to sign the Magna Carta. It had been drawn up by Stephen Langton. The complex document's 63 clauses reflect many of the barons' complaints against taxes and services to the king.

King John from a contemporary drawing by a monk.

? *Does it tell us what the artist thought was important about the king?*

CORE ACTIVITIES

1 What made John sign away some of his royal rights?
   - Try to answer this question by selecting 4 of the most likely reasons for the signing of Magna Carta from the following 8 statements:
     - John was aged 47 and growing sick and weary of fighting to keep his crown.
     - After many years of foreign wars, all his subjects hated the heavy taxation.
     - A group of barons rebelled because they were jealous of the king's friends who received land and pensions from him.
     - John was an energetic ruler who made sure his taxes, feudal dues and customs duties were collected and his courts were fairly and efficiently run.
     - John was vain and extravagant. He spent large sums on books, clothes and jewellery.
     - He probably murdered his nephew and heir, Arthur, in 1203.
     - He was defeated by the French and lost the duchy of Normandy in 1205.
     - He quarrelled with the Pope over the choice of Stephen Langton as Archbishop of Canterbury. England was punished by the Pope who banned all church services for five years.
     (*CLUE TO SUCCESS*: Feudal dues are payments made to the king by all landowners)

2 Read **A**.
   - What do the points listed there tell us about the grievances of the rebels in 1215?
   - How did the barons intend to make John keep his promise?

C

It was the first written programme of political reform ever imposed on an English king by his subjects.

The Companion to Medieval England. N. Saul, 1983.

D

In 1215 Magna Carta was a failure. It was intended as a peace and it provoked war.

Magna Carta. J.C. Holt, 1969.

E

A symbol of freedom, although it was largely intended to protect the privileges of the nobility.

Who's Who in History. W. Hassall, 1960.

EXTENSION ACTIVITY

1 **C**, **D** and **E** are comments made by modern historians.
   - Discuss each of these statements.
   - Why do you think Magna Carta has become the symbol of freedom for every citizen under English law?

F

Within three months of King John signing Magna Carta, civil war had begun again.

7. WOMEN IN THE MIDDLE AGES

Targets

* To investigate and explain the role of women in medieval society.
* To identify similarities and differences between the situation of women today and in the past.

1000
1100
1200
1300
1400
1500
1600
1700
1800
1900
2000

Most women in the Middle Ages were considered to be socially inferior to men. A wife was expected to stay at home cooking, cleaning and looking after the children.

When she married, a woman's property passed to her husband. The wife of a slave or serf belonged not only to her husband but also her lord. If land was involved, marriages were arranged regardless of the partners' feelings towards each other. Often the girl was as young as 14.

In the upper classes men took all the important decisions, managed their estates and went to war. The lord's lady was left to look after the family and manage the household. She could have a good deal of influence when her husband was absent for long periods.

Some women did become large landowners in their own right. A widow was entitled to a third of her husband's property as well as her dowry (money or land given by the bride's father to the bridegroom). Sometimes there was no male heir and a lord's daughter inherited both title and land.

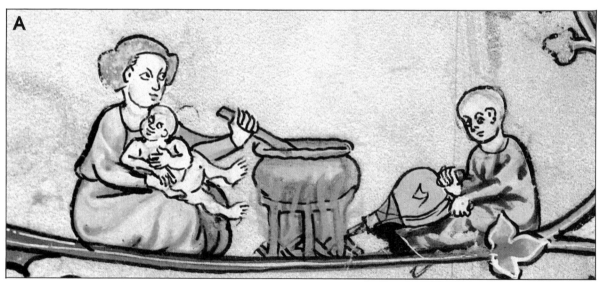

A

A woman nursing a baby and cooking.

Women in the lower classes

For the wives and daughters of peasants every day meant hard work. Their jobs included caring for large families, cooking, cleaning, washing, spinning, mending, combing out wool or flax, milking the cow, feeding the livestock, making cheese, gardening, helping in the fields with sowing, reaping, binding, threshing and ploughing.

Those who remained unmarried might work for their own family or in a lord's household. In some ways these were more self-sufficient and had greater equality than women in the upper classes, despite the endless toil.

A lady keeping an eye on the servant.

 *How is the life of this woman different to the one shown in **A**?*

A woman weaving.

Let her go often into the fields to see how they are working ... and let her make them get up in the morning. If she be a good housewife, let her rise herself ... go to the window and shout until she sees them come running out, for they are given to laziness ... show your folk that you know about it all and care about it, for so they will be the more diligent (hard working).

'The Goodman of Paris', 1393.

The duties of a good wife according to a Medieval book.

Women in towns

It was possible to become an apprentice and learn a trade which gave the woman a chance of independence. The most common occupations were jobs like spinning and weaving. Some moved into trade as cloth sellers, shopkeepers, tailors and even blacksmiths. It was not unusual for women to brew beer and run ale houses.

Widows frequently carried on their husband's business while some married women had occupations entirely separate from their spouses.

Healers and witches

Men were opposed to the idea of women as doctors, so few women actually qualified.

Most people knew a local 'wise woman' who could help to cure minor illnesses. She would have some remedies based on herbs and other natural medicines. Poor people could not afford the services of a doctor, so knowledge of setting broken bones, reducing high temperatures and even charming warts away often belonged to this old lady. Women also acted as 'midwives'. They had no qualifications but plenty of experience.

Remedies offered to the sick were often dependent on faith in the healer rather than any goodness contained in the medicine. Today faith healing is a respectable idea; in the Middle Ages it was easy to link it to spells and magic known only to witches. If a cure went wrong, then the patient's family could easily blame the 'witch'. Laws were harsh and the poor woman could be drowned or burnt to death.

21

Hospitals

Several hundred hospitals were set up in England during the Middle Ages. Some were attached to monasteries; others were built in towns to look after lepers, the insane or sick people generally. The nurses were often nuns. Women were also employed as servants, cooks and cleaners.

Helping to kill a pig.

 Why is the woman saving the blood?

F

A hospital worker of the C15th.

 What job do you think she did?

Women in the Church

There were no female priests or bishops. A nun could become quite important as the head of a convent. However, there were few large nunneries and there was no chance that a king or archbishop would choose a mere woman to be his leading adviser.

Upon her entry into a nunnery, the novice's family paid a dowry in recognition of her 'marriage to Christ'. Such sums were less than a normal dowry. However, she had to be provided with clothes and simple furniture. Becoming a nun was not a soft option for women even though it might seem better than being in the control of a husband or father.

A day in the life of a nun

Religious services began at 2 a.m. with Matins and Lauds. After a brief nap the nun returned to church at 6 a.m. The seven daily services ended with Compline at 8 p.m. Some nuns were so tired they slept through these sessions.

For about five hours a variety of tasks were carried out. Some older nuns trained the novices. Farming, spinning, making candles, managing the servants and the accounts, nursing in the infirmary and shopping in the local market were among the other jobs.

The novices were expected to learn to read Latin and French. Convents became increasingly important as schools for the children of the wealthy.

The size of the nunnery determined the range of duties for each member. In the small convents the nuns did all their own cooking and cleaning. In the largest convents the abbess had responsibilities similar to a powerful lord with an estate and a household to manage, involving many servants, farmworkers and tenants.

A convent would offer shelter to travellers and hospitality to the widows and wives of wealthy men who were serving in the king's army. In hard times the poor also looked to the religious houses for alms.

*Illustration of Chaucer's Prioress.
Geoffrey Chaucer described a prioress who was on a pilgrimage to the shrine of St. Thomas Becket.*

G

Her way of smiling was very simple and coy ...
And well she sang a service, with a fine
Intoning through her nose, as was most seemly,
And she spoke daintily in French, extremely ...
Pleasant and friendly in her ways, and straining
To counterfeit a courtly kind of grace,
A stately bearing fitting to her place,
And to seem dignified in all her dealings.

The Canterbury Tales. Chaucer, 1400.

CORE ACTIVITIES

1 Look carefully at **A**, **B**, **C** and **D**.
   ● What do they tell us about the knowledge a wife was supposed to have?

2 Look at the other information in this unit.
   ● How would you describe the attitude of men towards women in this period?
   ● What were the similarities and differences between poor and rich married women in terms of their opportunities to:
     - decide their future?
     - manage the work of other people?
   ● Make a list of the range of tasks carried out by ordinary women.
   ● How did girls learn how to do these jobs?

EXTENSION ACTIVITIES

1 Imagine you were the daughter of a rich man.
   ● Would it be better to marry a lord, or become a nun?
   ● Try to list the good and bad points about each.
   ● Which gave the woman more freedom and control of her own life?

2 Look at **G**.
   ● Using your dictionary if necessary, try to translate Chaucer's comments about the prioress into more simple English.

3 Think about the work of a nun.
   ● Which of the jobs done by nuns are carried out by other organisations or groups in our society today?

4 Look through this unit again.
   ● Write about the main differences between life for women then and now.
   ● What similarities can you find between the lives of women in the Middle Ages and today?

8. THE MEDIEVAL CHURCH

Targets

* To investigate the importance of the Church in the lives of people in the Middle Ages.
* To consider the experiences and viewpoints of monks and nuns.

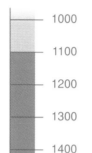

```
1000
1100
1200
1300
1400
1500
1600
1700
1800
1900
2000
```

It is difficult for us to understand how important the Christian Church was to everyone living in the Middle Ages. Belief in God was as natural as breathing. Everybody had to attend church services each Sunday and Holy Day. If you had a problem, the first thing to do was to pray. Each craft and occupation had its patron saint: St. Nicholas protected sailors, bakers had St. Honore while St. Christopher looked after travellers. The Virgin Mary comforted and forgave everyone, whatever their sins or weaknesses.

The Church gave meaning and purpose to life. This world was seen only as a preparation for the next, where the faithful would have an eternal home. Only a few could achieve salvation (entry into heaven) - perhaps one in a thousand. Since nobody knew who the lucky ones were, only one thing was certain: non-believers went to Hell.

These wall paintings have survived from the Middle Ages in the parish church at Pickering in North Yorkshire.

 What do you think is happening in this scene?

We can see images of Satan's kingdom in pictures and stained glass windows from the time. Remember the inside walls of churches were filled with paintings of saints or scenes from the Bible.

In the 'Canterbury Tales', Geoffrey Chaucer describes a Pardoner who made his living by selling pardons which he brought from the Head of the Church, the Pope in Rome. Such documents impressed both priests and ordinary people who were willing to pay as much as they could afford to gain forgiveness direct from Christ's representative on Earth.

B

'On one short day, in money down, he drew
More than the parson in a month or two,
And by his flatteries and prevarication
Made monkeys of the priest and congregation.'

From a modern translation of The Canterbury Tales.

 What does this tell us about a Pardoner?

Sinners faced fire, ice, darkness and pain forever. What power the priest had if he could hear your confession and forgive all your sins, giving you the chance to enter Heaven!

There were some sins which were difficult to avoid if you had certain jobs. For example, bankers sinned when they lent money and received interest on it. Merchants could buy a dispensation (forgiveness) from the Church if they traded with Muslims or received stolen goods. This was a kind of legal immunity for breaking the Church's law.

The Medieval Tithe Barn at Bradford-on-Avon, Wiltshire.

Giving charity to the Church in land or money was an act of generosity but it could also be a way of paying a penance for your sins. Certainly every rich person saw this as part of their Christian duty. In each village the parish priest had a patch of land called a glebe to farm. Of course churches were built and maintained with the help of such donations. In any case everyone had to pay a tithe or tenth part of their income to the Church. This could be in kind - crops or livestock. The great tithe barns which still survive remind us how large a store of wealth the Church must have had.

CORE ACTIVITIES

1 Look at the information on these pages.
  ● Try to list three reasons why the Church was so important to people in Medieval England.

2 Now look at **B**. The third line suggests that the pardoner flattered the people and also lied to them about how good his pardons would be in getting rid of their sins.
  ● Why did he do this?
  ● What made him such an unpopular figure at the time?

Life in a monastery

Monasteries formed a very important part of the Church in medieval England and Wales. They remind us that some men and women felt that they had to withdraw from the world to some extent in order to spend their time in prayer and working for their own community.

This did not mean that they had no contact with other people. If you were fortunate to live near a monastery then the help of the Church was very apparent. As well as acting as better landlords than many barons, monks provided charity, medical care and even credit to those who lacked the cash to buy seed or fodder in a bad season. Hospitality to travellers and education to some children, including the sons of the poor, might also be offered.

Who were the monks?

There were several types or orders each with its own rules and habits (gowns). For example, the Benedictines wore black and the Cistercians, who set up 75 abbeys in England, had white habits. Of course they all spent a great deal of time at prayer. The church was at the heart of every monastery.

Lay brothers were labourers who were not as educated as monks and did not wear habits. They attended the services and shared in all tasks of the abbey and its estate. Somtimes they were fugitives who had taken sanctuary in the abbey.

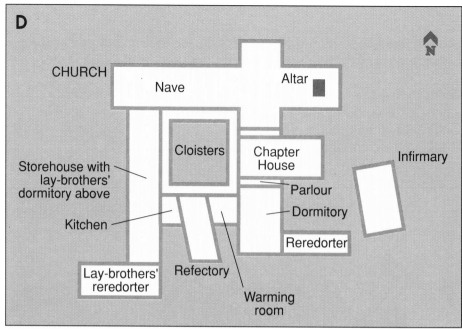

A plan of a monastery. The reredorter was a long narrow toilet.

A Monk's Day

2.30 a.m.	Matins (the first service).
Dawn	Prime followed by reading in the cloister.
8 a.m.	Wash, light breakfast. Tierce.
9 a.m.	Chapter meeting followed by work.
Noon	High Mass and dinner.
2.30 p.m.	Reading and work.
5 p.m.	Vespers and supper.
6 p.m.	Compline (the last service).
7 p.m.	Bed.

Each service had its own Latin name.

A ruined abbey.

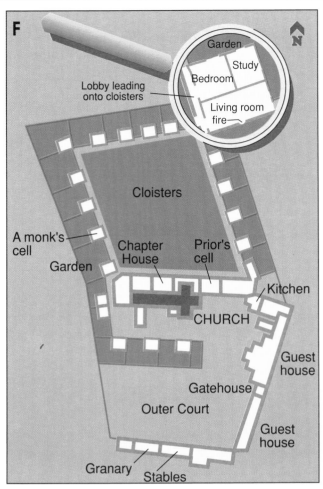

Plan of a Carthusian Abbey.

The Carthusians

The Carthusians were a very strict order. These monks were rarely allowed to speak. They spent most of their time in separate cells - two storey cottages each with its own vegetable garden, running water and flush toilet. Food was prepared by lay brothers and left in an L- shaped hatch in the wall so the monk could not see who brought it. They worked on weaving, making furniture or copying books. Although they met for regular services in the church they could not talk.

3 Look at **D**.
 ● What was the purpose of each area?

4 You will need a copy of **E**, which shows a ruined abbey.
 ● Label it in the same way as **D** to identify the same parts again.

5 Look at **D** and **F** together.
 ● What are the main differences between the two?
 ● Can you explain them?

A room in a Carthusian cell. The cell was stone built and contained plain wooden furniture and an open fire.

 How comfortable do you think life would have been in this cell?

EXTENSION ACTIVITIES

1 Today the Church of England does not have a 10% income tax to pay for all its costs.
 ● How is the work of the various Christian churches paid for?
 ● Discuss this in a small group.
 ● Present your ideas to the class. You may be able to invite a vicar or priest into school to tell you about this.

2 Imagine you are a traveller visiting a medieval monastery. You are welcomed and given hospitality by the abbot.
 ● Write an account of a typical day in a monastery, as seen through your eyes.

3 Think about the educated and wealthy people of this time.
 ● Apart from being very religious, what might have attracted such a person to become a monk or a nun?

9. DEVELOPMENT OF THE CASTLE

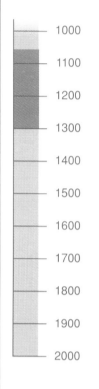

1000
1100
1200
1300
1400
1500
1600
1700
1800
1900
2000

Target

* To understand changes in castle design and purpose.

What do you think of when you hear the word 'castle'? Is it a fairy tale fortress with towers and fluttering flags or a real building you have seen?

Castles changed greatly during the Middle Ages for a variety of reasons.

The Motte and Bailey Castle

To keep control of the country they had won at Hastings, the Normans built 'motte and bailey' castles. Hilltops had been fortified since prehistoric times but King William needed to place his strongholds close to the people he wished to control. So, each large town had a castle to dominate it. If there was no hill nearby a mound of earth and stones was made with a wooden tower on the top.

The fence and moat around the bailey provided a first line of defence. Usually it contained a hall, chapel, an armoury, stables, workshops and bakehouses. The castle was almost a self-contained community.

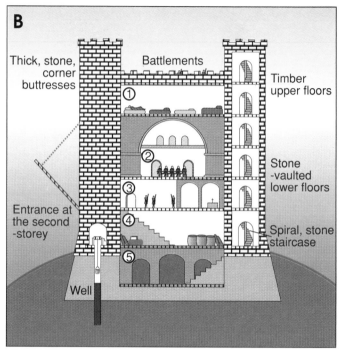

B — Thick, stone, corner buttresses — Battlements — Timber upper floors — ① — ② — Stone-vaulted lower floors — ③ — Entrance at the second-storey — ④ — Spiral, stone staircase — ⑤ — Well

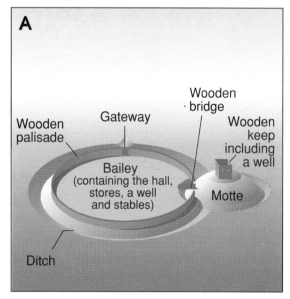

A — Wooden palisade — Gateway — Wooden bridge — Wooden keep including a well — Bailey (containing the hall, stores, a well and stables) — Motte — Ditch

A motte and bailey castle.

 In time, stone replaced wood as the main building material. What were the advantages of this do you think?

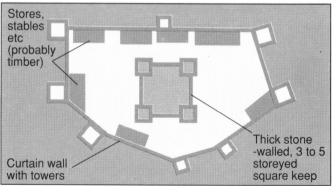

Stores, stables etc (probably timber) — Curtain wall with towers — Thick stone-walled, 3 to 5 storeyed square keep

Cross section of a square keep. This was the heart of the castle where the lord and his family lived.

 In the cross section 5 parts are not labelled. Can you suggest what each might have been used for?

The Square Keep

In time the wooden towers and walls were rebuilt with stone. Some lords erected large square keeps. These could accommodate the lord's family, servants and soldiers and be used to defend the castle if necessary.

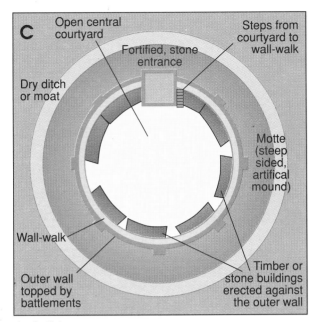

A shell keep.

The Shell Keep

After 1100 some castles were expanded to link the keep with the surrounding walls, making a kind of shell on top of the mound. The circular shape meant that soldiers could see attacks from any direction. The weakest point in any castle is the gateway. So, gatehouses were strongly built with towers each side of the drawbridge and portcullis (a heavy grating which slides up and down).

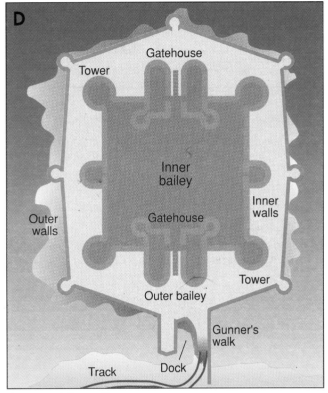

A concentric castle.

The Concentric Castle

As weapons improved castles had to change to meet different challenges. The Crusades brought fresh ideas for castle building. In the 13th century the first concentric castles were built, especially in Wales by Edward I. The basic idea is one ring of defence inside another. Sometimes there were three rings; the attackers might find that after breaking through one wall they were caught in a narrow area where the defenders could rain down arrows, spears and hot pitch on their heads. Of course it was even better if the castle was surrounded by a wide moat or on the coast.

CORE ACTIVITIES

1 Read the section The Motte and Bailey Castle.
- What was the importance of the motte for defence?
- What was the importance of the bailey for defence?

2 Look closely at **B**.
- What does it tell us about life in a Norman keep?

EXTENSION ACTIVITIES

1 Look again at the diagrams in this unit.
- With a partner, discuss the main changes between the castles.
- What improvements were made?
- Which features remained the same?

2 Imagine the castle in **D** is under attack. This is before cannon and gunpowder became common in Europe.
- How might the attacking army go about capturing the castle?
  (CLUE TO SUCCESS: Consider how they might get over, under or through the walls*)*

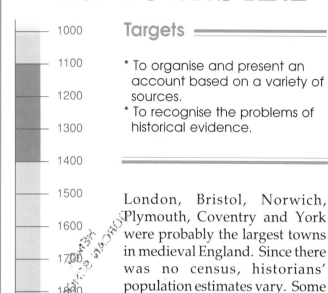

Targets

* To organise and present an account based on a variety of sources.
* To recognise the problems of historical evidence.

London, Bristol, Norwich, Plymouth, Coventry and York were probably the largest towns in medieval England. Since there was no census, historians' population estimates vary. Some indication of the relative size can be seen in this table which gives the amount of tax paid by certain towns to Edward III in 1334.

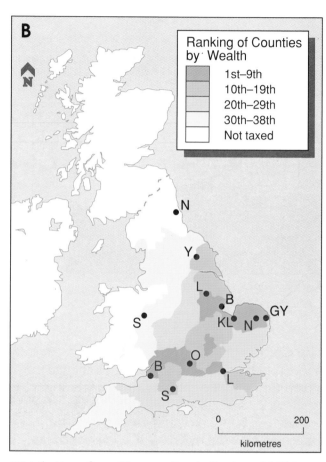

*Distribution of wealth according to the tax of 1334. The counties are placed in rank order according to the amount of tax paid. The letters locate the towns in **A**.*

A

Newcastle	£ 1 333
York	£ 1 620
Lincoln	£ 1 000
Boston	£ 1 100
King's Lynn	£ 770
Norwich	£ 946
Great Yarmouth	£ 1 000
Shrewsbury	£ 800
Oxford	£ 914
Bristol	£ 2 200
London	£11 000
Salisbury	£ 750

Edward III's subsidy (tax) of 1334. Sums paid by some major towns.

By 1500 historians estimate that London had a population of 50 000, five times bigger than any other English town.

Most of these towns dated back to Roman or Saxon times. Others grew quickly after the Norman Conquest. The lord would encourage settlement with a market near his castle in order to tax the traders. About 140 such towns appeared between 1100 and 1300. Sometimes a monastery provided employment and bought surplus food from the village. Coventry began in this way and became a major cloth centre. The export of wool and cloth dominated England's trade with Europe for centuries.

York: A Medieval City

If we put together some pieces of evidence about one of the largest cities, it may be possible to build up a picture of what a visitor might have seen and learnt about life there.

C

*The stone version of Clifford's Tower, built in 1245.
Its battlements and roof have disappeared.*

D

The city walls and the Minster.

E

The archbishop's diocese covered most of northern England. His own Minster church was one of 40 inside the city walls. There were also three monasteries, four friaries and a priory. These strong, high stone buildings and their numerous priests and lay clergy were very visible signs of the Church's influence over the citizens.

Written by a modern historian.

F

It was a very busy port, exporting wool, cloth and lead in exchange for wine and spices. The Company of Merchant Adventurers controlled the cloth trade as well as most of the foreign imports. It was the largest of over 50 such guilds or companies: craftsmen and merchants who had the right to vote in local elections and controlled the City Council.

Written by a modern historian.

G

The Great Hall of the Merchant Adventurers, built c.1368.

H

The Shambles, here butchers lived and traded.

I

The smell from slaughter houses was awful, especially in high summer. You had to walk across rough cobbles between bits of offal and stagnant puddles. The risk of slops being thrown out of bedroom windows was almost as bad as the danger of being mugged in these gloomy lanes at night.

Around the corner in the main market villagers brought their produce to sell. Many townsfolk grew their own crops in fields beyond the walls but it was good to have a better choice. Rats and dogs sniffed around the refuse each evening; disease spread quickly in the overcrowded houses which lacked running water.

Written by a modern historian.

J

On Corpus Christi day the guilds performed 48 'mystery' plays along a special route around the city. Each portrayed biblical scenes on a 'pageant wagon' pulled by workers.

Written by a modern historian.

CORE ACTIVITIES

1 Think carefully about the information on these pages.
   ● Which groups of people do you think had most influence upon the City of York?
   ● Explain your answer.

2 Look at **E**, **F**, **I** and **J**. They were all written by modern historians.
   ● Which provide:
     - facts?
     - impressions?
     - a mixture of both?

3 Now look at the photographs in this unit.
   ● How accurate or useful do you think they are in giving us information about York as it was 600 years ago?

A mystery play.

Monk Bar, one of five gateways.
Each had a stout oak portcullis with iron
spikes.

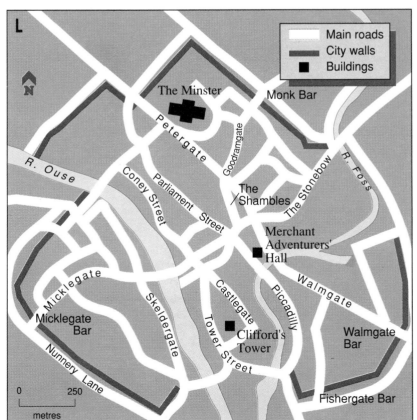

A map of medieval York.

Main roads
City walls
Buildings

The Minster
Monk Bar
Petergate
Goodramgate
R. Foss
R. Ouse
Coney Street
Parliament Street
The Shambles
The Stonebow
Merchant Adventurers' Hall
Walmgate
Micklegate
Skeldergate
Castlegate
Piccadilly
Micklegate Bar
Tower Street
Clifford's Tower
Walmgate Bar
Nunnery Lane
Fishergate Bar

0 250
metres

EXTENSION ACTIVITIES

1 Using all the evidence in this unit:
 ● Write a description of 'A walk
   around medieval York'.
 ● You could include details of your
   route, the sights, sounds and
   smells, the traffic, people and
   buildings. You can choose a visit
   today or in the Middle Ages.

2 If you wanted to find out how typical
  York was, compared to other towns in
  medieval England, how would you do
  it?
 ● List the questions you might
   ask and the kinds of evidence
   you would find helpful.

11. THE CRUSADES

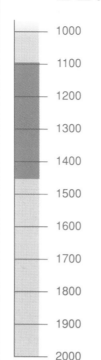

1000	
1100	
1200	
1300	
1400	
1500	
1600	
1700	
1800	
1900	
2000	

Targets

* To investigate events over a long period of time.
* To identify aspects of change and continuity.

Medieval maps often placed the Holy City of Jerusalem at the centre of the world. For Christians a pilgrimage there ensured entry into heaven. However, since 637 AD the Holy Land had been ruled by Muslims.

1095: The pope called on the rulers of Christendom to unite in a holy war to free Jerusalem from the Turkish Muslims.

1096: The First Crusade began. In the spring the preacher, Peter the Hermit, led a ramshackle peasant army which was wiped out by the Turks. Soon a better force, led by Godfrey de Bouillon, set off. Knights and nobles but no kings took part.

1099: The Crusaders captured the Holy City. Some stayed to establish the Kingdom of Jerusalem in the name of the pope.

1147: The Turks began to regain land so the second Crusade was launched, led by Louis VII of France and Konrad III of Germany. There were quarrels between the leaders and it failed.

1187: A new strong leader, Salah-ad-Din, united the Muslims and recaptured Jerusalem. The third and largest Crusade was organised, led by Emperor Frederick Barbarossa of Germany, Philip of France and Richard I of England.

1191: After many difficulties, the key port of Acre was taken. However, quarrels weakened the expedition and two attacks on Jerusalem failed. Christians were permitted to visit the Holy City and to trade generally in the Holy Land.

1200 - 1250: Four more crusades all failed. The military orders of the Templars and the Hospitallers did most of the fighting. Although the Holy Land remained under Muslim control the Crusades slowed down the movement of the Islamic peoples further into Europe for 350 years.

1453: The Turks captured the great city of Constantinople and Christian influence in the whole area was reduced.

A

A portrait thought to be of Salah-ad-Din, by an Egyptian artist.

CORE ACTIVITY

1 The following statements are about the Crusades.
- The leaders of the First Crusade were French nobles who wanted adventure and to win land and titles. One of them became king of Jerusalem.
- The king of England sometimes encouraged barons to go on a crusade so he would feel safer at home.
- By the year 1200 there were 100 000 Christians in the Holy Land. Very few mixed with or learnt about the culture of Muslims.
- 'Taking the cross' brought freedom for serfs.
- Monasteries frequently purchased land sold by crusaders to finance their expeditions.

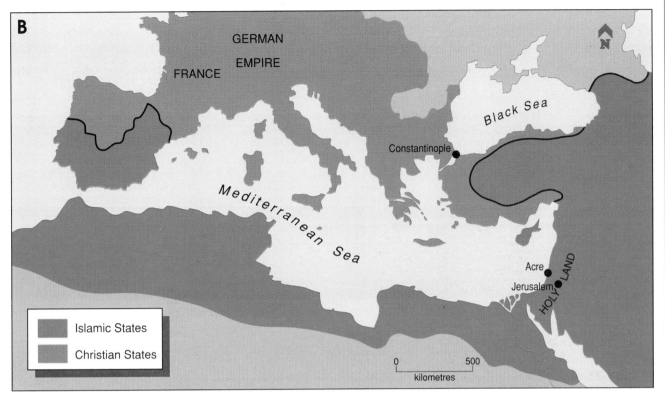

The Mediterranean lands in 1096.

- Trade with the east increased and new products like silk, damask, spices, perfumes, sugar and porcelain raised living standards in the west.
- Contact with different forms of Christianity and other beliefs encouraged new attitudes towards the pope and the Church in western Europe.
- The Crusades encouraged the ideals of chivalry when a knight vowed to protect the weak, honour women and fight for his faith.
- The Crusades increased hatred of non-Christians whether Muslim or Jew. Some of these people were even killed in England with the excuse that this was part of the Holy War.
- The pope who preached the first Crusade was anxious to show he was more powerful than a rival pope.

● Decide which are motives for crusading and which are the results of the Crusades.
● Make two separate lists, one for motives and another for results.

EXTENSION ACTIVITY

1 You will need a copy of the map, **B**.
  ● On it mark the route taken by King Richard the Lionheart on the third Crusade. He started his journey from London and finally reached Acre 19 months later.
  ● You will need an atlas to find these places:
    - Paris
    - Marseilles
    - Sicily
    - Crete
    - Cyprus
    - Acre
  ● Give your map an appropriate title.
  ● How did he get back home to England? *(CLUE TO SUCCESS*: Your school library may be a useful place to start)

12. ORIGINS OF PARLIAMENT

1000
1100
1200
1300
1400
1500
1600
1700
1800
1900
2000

Targets

* To recognise motivational factors and support with evidence.
* To identify an important turning point.

Saxons

Even though the word parliament was not used until the 13th century, our parliament has its beginnings as far back as Saxon times.

A

The chief men in the country were called Thanes, and the greatest of these were the earls. The earls helped the king to rule the country; they rode about with him, went hunting with him and acted as his bodyguard. When they met to give the king advice or sometimes to choose a new king, they were known as the Witan. This means a meeting of the wise men.

From Cavemen to Vikings. R.J. Unstead, 1974. A school history book.

? *Do you think the Witan was a powerful group of people? Give reasons for your answer.*

A Saxon king and the Witan.

? *What can you learn about the power of the Witan from **A**?*

King Alfred the Great

King Alfred, who reigned from 871 - 899, quickly realised the importance of the Witan. He needed advice from the men of the Witan, as well as help to raise armies to fight the Vikings. Alfred also realised that the Witan was a place where he could show that he was governing the country well. The laws he made gained authority as these were made with the advice of the Witan.

1066: The Norman Conquest

After William the Conqueror had won the Battle of Hastings and became King of England, he continued the tradition of calling his important subjects together.

William called together his Great Council at the time of religious festivals, such as Christmas, Easter and Whitsun. Even so, William was still the most powerful person in the land. It was his decision whether or not the council was called. He gave the Saxon lands to his own chief followers in return for an oath in which they promised to fight for William. These chief followers then gave some of the land to their own men who also swore an oath to the baron. So land was held in return for services. This is called the feudal system.

C

1085: The king spent Christmas with his councillors at Gloucester, and held his court there for five days...the king had important deliberations and discussions with his council about this land, how it was peopled and with what sort of men.

The Anglo-Saxon Chronicle. Written at the time.

D

Medieval king talking to his council of advisers.

⚠? *Can you identify the different types of people involved in this council?*

Henry II

Henry II reigned from 1154 to 1189 and was king of a huge empire, which included half of France, England, Ireland and Wales. He realised that a system of government was needed so that the country would be run properly when he was away in other parts of the empire. He set up a system of lawyers and clerks who remained at Westminster when he travelled abroad.

The feudal system had given great power to the barons and they disliked the new royal civil service which Henry established.

After Henry's death in 1189 his son Richard came to the throne. Richard was rarely in England, but spent his time fighting abroad. His wars meant that the clerks at Westminster had to tax people heavily.

Magna Carta

When John came to the throne after Richard's death, he found that there were many outstanding debts for Richard's wars. John was not a good king and his barons made him sign the Magna Carta.

E

> To get the general consent of the Kingdom for the size of an aid (tax) ...we order the archbishops, bishops, abbots, earls and greater barons to be called by letter sent to each one.
>
> *Magna Carta. 1215.*

The Magna Carta was an important document in the history of parliament because it stated that the king could not impose new taxes without calling the 'Common Council of the Realm'. Although John did not abide by the Magna Carta, after his death the charter continued to be issued to kings.

Simon de Montfort

King John's son, Henry III, also had problems raising money. He argued with the barons and refused to talk with them about taxes. The leader of the barons was a man called Simon de Montfort. After defeating Henry III in battle in 1264, Simon became the virtual ruler of England.

F

> De Montfort ... called a Parliament, including a number of commoners, to adminster the country, probably the first time townsmen were summoned in Parliamentary history.
>
> *History of England. John Burke, 1974.*

 What was unusual about Simon's parliament?

Simon was the first person to use the word parliament. It came from the French word parlement which means to speak or talk. However, some of his ideas were too new. The barons did not like townsmen being involved in a parliament. In 1265 Simon was defeated in battle, but his ideas were not forgotten, particularly by Henry III's son, Edward I.

Parliaments of the C14th and C15th.

1300s: Barons became known as Lords. They were summoned to Parliament by royal writ. Each borough or shire also sent 2 representatives.

Parliament sat at the Royal Court. No one knew how long a Parliament might last.

During 1300s: Knights and burgesses joined together to form the House of Commons.

The Earls and Barons stayed in the Council Chamber with the King and eventually formed the House of Lords.

Throughout 1300s: Problems and disagreements between various kings and Parliaments continued.

1399: Henry IV took the throne from Richard II with Parliament's support. Henry agreed to Parliament having freedom of speech.

1406: Law passed giving all freemen of a county the right to vote, but in ....

1430: Commons limited the vote to Forty-Shilling Freeholders (a man who owned land worth forty shillings or more). This meant that only very wealthy people could vote.

1400s: Parliament influenced by nobles. This was a century of violence and bribery. During the Wars of the Roses, Parliament often changed sides.

1485: Henry Tudor defeated Richard III and began to revive Parliament, mainly so they could confirm his right to the throne.

1487: Star Chamber Act passed. This set up a special court to deal with offences committed by wealthy men. However, once he was established on the throne he rarely called Parliament.

Edward I and his parliament.

 Can you spot any similarities between this parliament and our parliament today?

Edward I

In 1295 Edward summoned a parliament which included barons, clergy, knights and burgesses (wealthy townspeople). This became known as the 'Model Parliament' and set the pattern for future parliaments. Even so, Edward still thought of parliament as being there to raise money for him. However, in return he did allow it to help with the passing of some laws.

CORE ACTIVITIES

1 Use these pages to find out about:
  - Saxons
  - King Alfred
  - William the Conqueror
  - Henry II
  - Simon de Montfort
  - Edward I
  - Henry IV
  - Henry Tudor
- For each:
  - say why the king called together a council or parliament
  - support your answer with evidence
  - try to suggest what the effect was of kings calling the council or parliament

2 Choose **one** event in the history of parliament which you think was an important *turning point*.
- Say which it is, and give reasons for your choice.

EXTENSION ACTIVITIES

1 Working with some friends:
- Design a diagram to show the development of parliament. Use this unit, together with any other information you can find, to help you.

2 You will need a sketch of **H**.
- Try to find out who the different people shown might be.
- Label them on your own copy of the picture.

3 Look again at **G**.
- What do you think is meant by 'freedom of speech'?
- Find out how much 40 shillings would be worth today.

13. EDWARD I AND THE WELSH

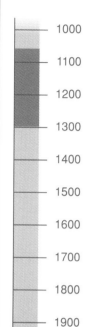

| 1000 |
| 1100 |
| 1200 |
| 1300 |
| 1400 |
| 1500 |
| 1600 |
| 1700 |
| 1800 |
| 1900 |
| 2000 |

Targets

* To investigate changes over varied time periods.
* To consider how the decisions of leading individuals are influenced by long term developments.

Wales is a land of hills and mountains, surrounded on three sides by the sea. Any invader has to be prepared to send columns of soldiers into its long narrow wooded valleys, risking sudden attack. They must trudge up steep open hillsides where cold winds bite deep and storms sweep in from the sea.

Today Welsh people still have a strong sense of their Celtic origins, with its own language, music and literature. The Celts migrated to Britain from Europe around 2 000 B.C. bringing with them knowledge of metal tools and weapons. They constructed hill forts as secure homes.

The Romans never properly conquered the Welsh. It was only in the gentle vales of the south that they built a fort at Caerleon, a town at Caerwent and many villas. Christianity became the official religion of Roman Britain but most of the Welsh continued to worship spirits and gods in the natural world around them. The priests of the Celtic religion, the Druids, had great influence over each tribe.

After 500 A.D., Celtic Christian missionaries from Ireland began a very rapid conversion, founding monasteries, schools and churches across the whole country. The Welsh patron saint, David, was a leading priest in the 6th century.

The waves of invasions by Angles and Saxons were strongly resisted by the Welsh. Finally the Saxon king of Mercia, Offa, began to build a huge dyke, like a long moat. In 784, it became the traditional borderline with England.

The ruins of Castell-y-Bere. Built by Llywelyn the Great.

The Norman Conquest

After 1066 the new rulers of England posed the most serious threat ever faced by the Welsh. William I encouraged his lords to lead their knights into the valleys and set up strongholds to subdue the inhabitants. Over 100 motte and bailey castles appeared, mainly around the south coast and along the borders or 'marches'. At first they were wooden palisades on mounds; some became permanent stone fortresses which were enlarged and strengthened in the following centuries.

Henry I, who reigned from 1100 to 1135, was keen to make the population of Wales more obedient. He sent colonies of English and Flemish people to settle in walled towns across the south as far as Pembroke. There the character of the population changed so much that it became known as 'the little England beyond Wales'. The Norman lords who dominated these settlements behaved like petty kings, levying taxes, controlling law courts and even minting coins.

In the hills and mountains of central and north Wales the native tribes paid lip service to Norman rule and retained their customs, laws and way of life, based on pastoral farming. Their chiefs learnt from the Normans how to build their own castles and use new weapons and battle tactics. When the English kingdom was weakened by civil war or the absence of the king in foreign wars or crusades, they took the opportunity to seize back control from their Norman overlords.

Conway Castle, 1283.

Llywelyn the Great (1173-1240)

During Richard the Lionheart's reign, in 1194, a young prince set himself up as ruler of Gwynned, the mountainous area of Snowdonia. He joined with other Welsh princes or chiefs to resist English rule. Soon the idea of a united independent Wales took hold. At times Llywelyn found it helpful to say he was obedient to the English king and accept the right to rule most of Wales in his name. But the Marcher Lords, descendants of William the Conqueror's barons, were not prepared to accept a Welsh prince. The warfare ebbed back and forth. At the time of Llywelyn's death his principality of Gwynned seemed secure. Within seven years his successors had surrendered their independence to Henry III.

Llywelyn the Last gained a position of strength similar to that of his grandfather when he became sole ruler of Gwynned in 1255. Henry III was facing revolt from his barons so once again the Welsh were able to assert their independence. Henry was forced to recognise Llywelyn as 'Prince of Wales', lord of the whole of northern and central parts, by the treaty of Montgomery in 1267.

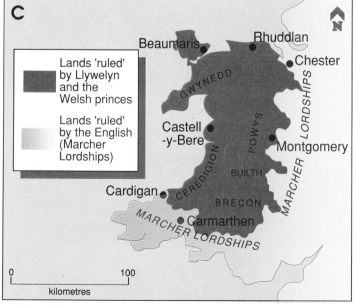

Wales after the Treaty of Montgomery, 1267.

The Prince of Wales versus the King of England

In 1272 a new strong king of England came to the throne. Edward I was 33 years old, an experienced warrior, tall, handsome and determined to show who really ruled in Wales.

Llywelyn failed to appear at court to do homage to Edward as his overlord. His patience exhausted, Edward decided to attack Gwynned in November 1276. Three separate armies marched into Wales while the English fleet cut off Llywelyn's corn supplies from Anglesey. The Prince's Welsh allies proved unreliable and Llywelyn soon sought peace terms. Edward divided up his lands but allowed Llywelyn to keep his title of prince.

The king also ordered the building of new castles at key points around Gwynned. Having been on a crusade and fought in France, Edward was an expert on the latest developments in fortification. He employed 3 000 men to begin constructing concentric castles which were like a Russian doll: one castle inside another so that the garrison could fall back to a second line of defence if necessary.

Llywelyn against Edward: Round Two

The speed of the castle building and the limits upon their power seem to have driven Llywelyn and his brother David into revolt in March 1282. The immediate cause lay in the issue of whether Welsh or

English law should be applied in a dispute over land. David's anger led him to attack a royal castle. This took both Llywelyn and Edward by surprise. Even though he probably saw the futility of the revolt, Llywelyn felt compelled to join it as the leader of his countrymen.

By August Edward was ready to invade once more. Again he used his fleet to control the northern coast and gathering his army at his new castle at Rhuddlan. He quickly marched west towards Anglesey, capturing Welsh strongpoints quickly.

Negotiations took place in which Llywelyn was offered an earldom and land in England if he would give up his princedom in Snowdonia.

Not surprisingly the Welsh were indignant at such a proposal which Edward probably knew they would refuse.

Beaumaris Castle, 1295.

Castle builders at work.

He prepared to invade the brothers' mountain stronghold in winter but Llywelyn's own impatience saved him the trouble. Keen to seek support in the south he marched to Builth Castle. He thought it would be poorly defended but he was surprised by a cavalry attack and his men fled. In the confusion the prince was run through by an English lance. His brother, David, was captured and executed after holding out until the following spring. Both their heads were displayed at the Tower of London. With them the last hopes of Welsh independence had also died.

1284: Making the defeat final
In a statute issued from his castle at Rhuddlan Edward announced the formation of new counties under royal control. Gwynned disappeared from the map.

F

Edward I.

The king's young son, Edward, was named as Prince of Wales, a title which has continued ever since for the first born son of every English monarch. This decision was very popular in Wales.

CORE ACTIVITIES

1 Look at the periods and dates below.
   43 - 410 AD
   500
   784
   1066 - 1135
   1194 - 1240
   1255 - 1267
   1276 - 1282
   1284
   ● For each of these write a brief comment about:
   - the main changes taking place
   - how independent Wales was at that time
   (CLUE TO SUCCESS:
   43 - 410 AD: The Romans only controlled South Wales. Christianity did not become established)
   ● Draw a timeline to show the course of Welsh history.

2 ● How did Edward I try to make sure the Welsh would not pose a serious threat to his rule again?

The most visible expression of royal power was the Edwardian castle. By 1296, 17 new castles had been built. Labour was recruited from all over England. James of St.George, a great castle architect from Italy, was made 'Master of the King's Works in Wales' for the generous salary of 15p per day.

The size and number of these castles were never matched again in British history. Situated near the sea and dominating adjacent towns, they showed the Welsh that the foreign rulers meant to stay. When a Welsh family, the Tudors, gained the English throne the Act of Union, in 1536, confirmed Edward I's victory by uniting the two countries in law.

EXTENSION ACTIVITIES

1 Today the Welsh language and literature remain important in the central and northern areas.
   ● What reasons can you find in this section for their survival?

2 ● What choices did Llywelyn the Last face in his attempts to keep his princedom independent? Was he bound to lose in the end?

3 ● Discuss with a friend how far both Llywelyn the Last and Edward were influenced by the history of relationships between English and Welsh rulers before their time.

14. ROBERT THE BRUCE

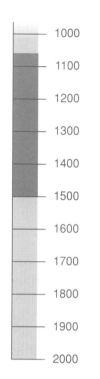

1000
1100
1200
1300
1400
1500
1600
1700
1800
1900
2000

Targets

* To describe the character and motives of Robert the Bruce.
* To assess his impact on Scottish history.

Up to 1040, when Macbeth came to the Scottish throne, Scotland had been a Celtic kingdom ruled by its own kings. However, Macbeth's successor Malcolm Canmore married Margaret, an English princess. She brought many English ways to Scotland.

After the Battle of Hastings, when William the Conqueror became King of England, landowners who refused to acknowledge him as king fled to Scotland to seek refuge with King Malcolm and Margaret. Henry I of England, the son of William the Conqueror, married the daughter of King Malcolm and this brought a period of peace between England and Scotland. Gradually the laws and customs of England were used in the lowlands of Scotland and there was a great deal of trade between the two countries. Although some of the Celtic people revolted against these English ways, Scotland eventually became more peaceful.

Many English kings had great influence in Scotland, but when Edward I came to the English throne in 1272 he was determined to have more than just influence. He wanted to become master of Scotland, Ireland and Wales.

Men practising with longbows.

Edward wanted a final say in Scottish affairs, so he chose a man whom he thought would listen to him. This man was John Balliol. However, the Scots refused to accept Edward's interference and rebelled against him. This gave Edward the excuse for a full scale invasion of Scotland.

A

When Edward first turned his attention to the Scots, he hoped for a peaceable union of the two countries (England and Scotland). Scotland had preserved a sturdy independence under a succession of kings skilled in controlling the rivalries of local chieftains, until in 1286 Alexander III was thrown over a cliff by his horse. His heiress was his granddaughter Margaret, the 'Maid of Norway', and although she was only a child Edward won approval for her marriage to his son. She set sail from Norway in 1290 but died on reaching Orkney, and Edward's dream of a personal union betwen the two crowns vanished. Edward was then asked by the Scots to be an impartial judge between a dozen claimants to their throne.

An Illustrated History of England. John Burke, 1974.

 Why do you think Edward wanted to marry his son to Margaret?

Edward invades Scotland

When Edward invaded Scotland he used the new longbows. These were about 1.5 metres in length and could fire arrows with such force that even armour could be pierced. Using these new weapons Edward defeated John Balliol in 1296.

On returning to England, Edward took with him the famous Stone of Destiny upon which Scottish kings had sat to be crowned for hundreds of years. Taking it away from Scotland was a terrible insult to the Scots.

One year later another uprising in Scotland, led by Sir William Wallace, was also defeated by Edward. Although Wallace escaped he was eventually captured in 1305 and put to death by being hung, drawn and quartered. His head was placed on a spike at London Bridge.

C

The seal of Robert the Bruce.

 How do you think this seal may have been used?

Six weeks later Robert had himself crowned King of Scotland at Scone where Scottish kings had been crowned for generations.

After being crowned Robert captured some Scottish castles which had been held by the English and many Scots people supported him, but gradually his family and supporters were captured by the English. Many of these Scottish lords were put to death and their lands given to English nobles by Edward.

Robert the Bruce, 1274 - 1329

One of the followers of William Wallace was a man called Robert Bruce. He came from one of the most important and wealthy clans in Scotland. At this time Robert was 31 years old and although he had sometimes supported Edward I, the dreadful way in which Wallace was put to death made Robert decide that Scotland should be ruled by a Scotsman without interference from English kings. In 1306 Robert decided to win the throne of Scotland for himself.

D

Another claimant was John 'The Red' Comyn, and in a quarrel within the sacred precincts of Greyfriars Church in Dumfries, Bruce killed him. Historians disagree as to the reason behind the deed. Some maintain Comyn was about to betray to the English king a joint plan of revolt. Others maintain it was just rivalry for the throne of Scotland. Some say Bruce did not strike the fatal blow, that it was done by his companions. Others...say Bruce had the dying man brought to him at the altar steps and there dispatched him (killed him). It seems likely that the killing was...the climax of a sudden quarrel.

100 Great Kings, Queens and Rulers of the World. Ian Fellowes-Gordon, 1973.

 Why do historians disagree about Robert Bruce's involvement in the death of John Comyn?

45

The legend of Robert the Bruce

Robert had no option but to hide in the Scottish highlands. By 1307 he was in exile on the Isle of Arran. It might have been at this time that a famous legend began.

Perhaps you have heard the story of Robert and the spider? One day, so the story goes, while sitting in a damp cave, feeling miserable because he could not defeat the English, Robert watched a spider. It was trying to spin a web but kept falling down to the ground. However, rather than giving up the spider went on and on until eventually it succeeded.

It is said that this made Robert realise that he had to keep on trying to defeat the English even though he had lost many battles. Perhaps this is where the saying 'If at first you don't succeed then try, try, try again' may come from. We have no historical evidence that this actually happened, but it is a story which has been passed on for generations.

1307 - 1314

For over a year Robert was hounded by the English, but in 1307 he defeated an English force at Loudoun Hill in Ayrshire. Edward I moved a large force of men northwards to meet Robert but Edward died in Carlisle before reaching Scotland.

The English throne passed to Edward's son who became Edward II. However, compared with his father he was a weak king. Instead of acting against Robert the Bruce immediately, Edward II left matters in Scotland to look after themselves.

Robert seized his opportunity and succeeded in taking every Scottish castle held by the English except for Stirling. Eventually in 1314 Edward II marched northwards to challenge Robert.

E

A Scottish Foot Soldier, based on a drawing from a manuscript, c.1307.

 What questions might you ask about this evidence?

The night before the battle

The two sides were not evenly matched. Edward II had about 17 000 men, 2 000 were knights on horseback, the other 15 000 foot soldiers and archers with longbows. Robert had an army of only 5 000 men.

On 23rd June the English forces arrived at Bannock Burn, hot and tired after marching 20 miles. Robert's forces were positioned on a small hill. They had dug pits between themselves and the English then covered the pits with grass to hide them. Despite their tiredness some of the English knights attacked the Scots, but were hampered by the pits and were pushed back.

That same night an English knight, Henry de Bohun, came across Robert who was checking the position of the English army. Seeing the possibility of killing Robert, Henry rode at the Scottish king.

F

Robert was mounted on a small hackney (pony) and held only a light battle-axe in his hand, but, warding off his opponent's spear, he cleft his skull with so terrible a blow that the handle of the axe was shattered in his grasp.

History of the English People. J.R. Green, 1892.

 What effect might Robert's defeat of Henry de Bohun have had on the English soldiers?

The Battle of Bannock Burn 24th June, 1314

On the morning of 24th June both armies faced each other. Robert's spearmen were in four tightly packed groups. The English had their backs to the small stream called Bannock Burn.

G

When both sides were ready to fight, the English archers were put in the front of the battle line. The Scottish archers fought with them and on both sides a few were killed and wounded ... Now when two armies had drawn close, all the Scots knelt to say the Lord's Prayer. After this they advanced boldly against the English ... Truthfully, when the armies clashed and the great horses of the English charged the pikes of the Scots as if into a dense forest, there arose a great and terrible sound of broken spears and fatally wounded war horses. So there was stalemate for a while. Now the English in the rear could not reach the Scots because the front line was in the way. Nor could they do anything themselves. Therefore there was nothing left but to flee. This story I heard from a man I can trust, who was an eyewitness.

An account written many years later.

Detail from a drawing made some time after the battle. Try to identify the English and the Scots. Give reasons for identification.

1314 - 1500

The defeat of the English at Bannock Burn firmly established Robert the Bruce as king of Scotland. In 1328 the Treaty of Northampton was signed by regents (people who rule for a king or queen who are too young to rule themselves) of Edward III. When he was old enough to rule England himself he decided to try to re-establish English influence in Scotland. This led to another period of war and conflict which continued for the next 200 years. It was not until 1707 that England and Scotland were legally joined by the Act of Union.

CORE ACTIVITIES

1 Look at the material in this unit.
  ● Describe the dress and weapons of the soldiers at this time.
  ● Include some drawings.

2 Working with a partner:
  ● Write a report describing the character and motives of Robert the Bruce. Use evidence from this unit to support your ideas.
  (CLUE TO SUCCESS: You should try to describe how he looked, what he might have worn, whether he was kind, cruel, friendly, brave or cowardly*)*
  ● Why do you think Robert behaved in the way he did?

3 Think about this period of time.
  ● What effect do you think Robert had on Scottish history at the time?

EXTENSION ACTIVITIES

1 Using this unit to help you:
  ● Write a report of the battle of Bannock Burn from the point of view of an English reporter OR a Scottish reporter.
  ● Make it clear which side you support.

2 Find out more about Scottish history at this time.
  ● You could work in a small group and display your findings on a wall chart or in a booklet.

15. THE BLACK DEATH

1000
1100
1200
1300
1400
1500
1600
1700
1800
1900
2000

Target

* To identify the causes and results of an event.

In the 1340s a disease known as the Black Death or the plague broke out in southern China. It was frightening because it spread very quickly and killed many people. The disease seemed to travel along the trade routes to Europe.   In September 1348 the first case was reported in England at Melbourne in Dorset. (Today the port is called Weymouth.) From there it spread eastwards to London and then throughout the land.

Historians think that about 2.5 million people died in Britain from the Black Death in the next two years. This means that about half the population were wiped out.

Before reading any further find a partner. In your note books write down - 1348 The Black Death. Now together make a list of all the historical questions you would ask about this title.

What was the Black Death?

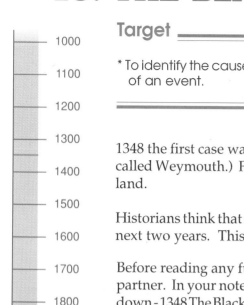

A

An excavation said to be the largest and most important in England is yielding a fascinating insight into the lives and deaths of Londoners during the Black Death, which killed nearly half the capial's population, up to 50 000 people, in the year 1349.

The dig, costing £1 million, is on the site of the old Royal Mint near the Tower of London, where more than 1 000 corpses are thought to be buried.

Archaelogists have uncovered orderly rows of graves which merge with a hastily filled gravel pit, made as the disease, bubonic plague, swept London.

Only one small metal belt clasp and traces of shrouds have been found in the graves.

Mr Peter Mills, field officer of the Museum of London, said yesterday: "We assume grave-diggers would help themselves to anything of value such as rings and brooches as a perk of the job and perks must have been few at the time".

The skeletons are being analysed to determine sex, height and age, and for any traces of arthritis, tuberculosis or other diseases.

They will then be re-buried in east London.

An archaeological excavation.
Now try to answer some of your questions using the information you have seen and read so far.

B

In men and women alike the plague first showed itself by the appearance of swellings in the groin (top of the leg) and armpits. Some as large as apples or eggs, some less. From these two parts of the body the boils spread in all directions and after this black spots appeared often on the arm or thigh.

A description of the Black Death in Florence, Italy. Written by a poet, Boccaccio, 1353.

What did people believe was the cause?

C

In some places it was believed that the Jews had poisoned the people ... In some quarters that it was the poor cripples and in others that it was the nobles (rich) ... the truth is that there were two causes ... (1) the close position of the three great planets, Saturn, Jupiter and Mars ... Such a coming together of planets is always a sign of wonderful, terrible or violent things to come ... (2) the state of the body - bad digestion, weakness and blockage, and for this reason people died.

Guy de Chauliac, a doctor who lived at the time of the Black Death.

D

Many wise people think that the Jews are not guilty of poisoning the water with plague and that the Jews only confessed to doing so because they were tortured. Wise people think that the plague was due to the great earthquake which took place in January of last year, 1348; this burst open the crust of the earth and allowed the bad, noxious poisons and vapours (mists) to enter the wells and springs ... A large proportion of Jews are doctors and they therefore know how to avoid the plague.

Helvetian Chronicle. Tschudi, c.1349.

E

The disease is sent from God as a punishment for our sins.

A priest, C14th.

Doctors were powerless against the disease. Many refused to see sick people in case they caught the disease themselves.

C, **D** and **E** *give several different causes of the Black Death.*

 Which of these do you think is the most likely cause?

How did people try to cure those with the disease?

F

For cures - bleeding and purges (something to clean out the stomach and bowels), cordials and medicinal powders can be used. The swelling should be softened with figs and cooked onions, peeled and mixed with yeast and butter, then opened and treated like ulcers.

Guy de Chauliac.

 How are these cures different from those we might try today?

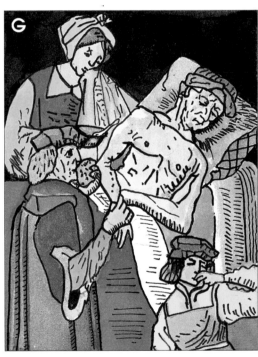

G

A doctor treating a dying man.

H

 Why do you think the doctor and lady are holding something to their noses?

49

What was the real cause of the Black Death?

Today we know that the disease was spread by the fleas which lived on black rats. A person became infected when bitten by one of these fleas. There was also a form of the disease which could be spread from one person to another.

It was possible for the Black Death to spread very rapidly. Although it died out in 1350 the plague often reappeared during the next 300 years.

I

Order to cause the human feces (bodily waste) and other filth lying in the streets and lanes of the city and its suburbs to be removed with all speed ... The king has learned how ... the air is infected and the city poisoned to the danger of men.

A message from King Edward III to the Lord Mayor of London, 1349.

Why was the disease likely to spread rapidly at that time?

J

Twigg puts forward the theory that anthrax may account for the many people who died from the Black Death. The symptoms of anthrax are very similar to bubonic plague ... Anthrax also kills farm animals ... It is transmitted from person to person and ... travels much faster than bubonic plague, the death rate was 90% ... plague only kills humans, rodents (rats) and monkeys.

Medieval England Teachers' Handbook. A report on the work of Graham Twigg, a modern zoologist. John Simkin, 1986.

 Can you find any evidence from the sources in this unit to support Twigg's theory that anthrax was the Black Death?

K

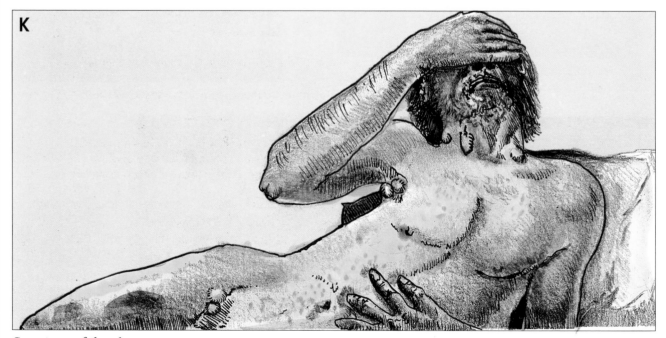

Symptoms of the plague.

The Black Death had a great effect on life after 1350. However, we have to be very careful about the conclusions we draw from the evidence. For example, some of the things which we think happened as a result of the disease might have happened even without it! Also we have to remember that not every part of England suffered from the disease. There are some general conclusions we can make.

L

England during the Black Death	Possible effects of the Black Death
▼ More than half the population of England died from the Black Death. ▼ There were fewer people to work on the land. ▼ Many tenants who worked the land of the lord of the manor died. ▼ Many skilled people, like stone masons, died. ▼ No one really knows what caused the disease.	▼ The lord of the manor started to keep sheep instead of growing crops. ▼ It took 300 years for the population of England to get back to the 1347 figure. ▼ Fewer churches were built. ▼ People were terrified of another outbreak of the Black Death. ▼ Wages for those who worked on the land increased.

EXTENSION ACTIVITIES

1 Working with your partner look back at the questions you wrote at the start of this unit.
   ● Try to answer as many of these as you can using the information in this unit.

2 You are going to write your own historical report on the disease.
   ● First you need to make a plan. You will see that each of the sections in this unit begins with a question. These are probably very like the ones you wrote down.
   ● Use each of these as a heading for your report. You can add any other questions of your own as extra headings.
   ● Under each heading try to answer the question by writing down what you can learn from the sources. You can also use any other books which may be available.
   ● Finally, add the following heading: 'The results of the Black Death'.
   ● Using **J** and **L** try to explain in your own words what might have happened in England during the years after the Black Death.

CORE ACTIVITY

1 Look at **L**. It shows two lists of statements. One describes England during the Black Death and the other lists possible effects.
   ● Make a list of the statements.
   ● Now decide which effect should be linked to each statement.

16. THE PEASANTS' REVOLT 1381

```
1000
1100
1200
1300
1400
1500
1600
1700
1800
1900
2000
```

Targets

* To investigate the causes of the Revolt.
* To show an understanding of different viewpoints by looking at the key decisions within a series of events.

The events of 1381

In 1381 the 14 year old King Richard II faced a serious rebellion by thousands of peasants who marched on London.

March: The King ordered the arrest of anyone refusing to pay the poll tax. John Ball was imprisoned by the Archbishop of Canterbury in Maidstone.

May: Riots broke out in Essex and Kent. Some tax collectors were murdered.

June 6: The peasant army in Kent captured Rochester Castle and chose Wat Tyler, a former soldier, as leader.

A

Richard II.

June 11: Under Tyler's command, they reached Blackheath, on the edge of London. They released John Ball from prison on the way. Meanwhile the Essex rebels were camped at Mile End, north of the Thames. Together they formed a force of approximately 50 000.

The causes

1

By 1350 the number of working people had been drastically reduced by the Black Death. Peasants were able to leave their villages and find higher wages elsewhere.

2

In 1351 Parliament passed the Statute of Labourers. This kept wages at the level of 1347. Any workers who did not accept low pay would be imprisoned.

3

Preachers such as John Ball, a priest in Kent, spread ideas of fairness and equality. He asked why a few should have riches and comfort while the majority had to suffer from long hours of labour, low wages and terrible living conditions. He referred to stories from the Bible which everyone knew to make his point: 'When Adam delved (dug) and Eve span, Who was then the gentleman?'

4

To pay for a war against France the King imposed a tax on every person over 15 regardless of their wages. This poll tax fell heavily upon poor peasants when it was increased twice in two years.

Four of the main causes for the revolt.

 What connections can you find between these causes? (CLUE TO SUCCESS: Look for a word beginning with 'w')

CORE ACTIVITIES

1 Read these events carefully.
- What tactics should Tyler follow at this stage? Remember events had moved very quickly and the king was not able to gather an army to face such a large attack. The peasants had to be fed and sheltered and the question was, 'How much time did Tyler have before they became impatient to attack the city'?

2 King Richard had taken refuge in the Tower but little had been done to organise the city's defences. His advisers probably knew that the peasants had plenty of support among the lower classes of London who, given the chance, might join in any attack on the property of the rich.
- What should he do?
- Discuss these points in your group and record your decision.
- Now read on to find out what actually happened.

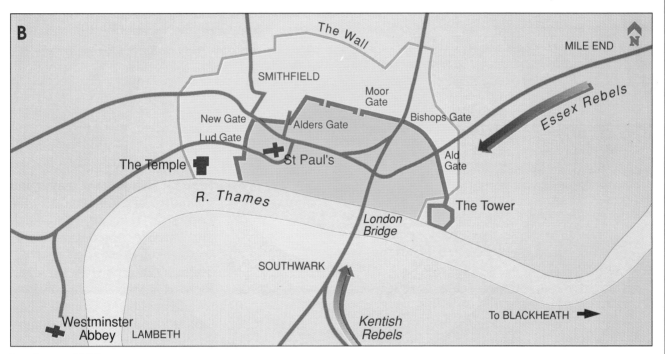

London in 1381.

June 13: The rebels sent a petition asking the king to execute his chief advisers but claiming to be loyal to Richard himself. The king and his chancellor, the Archbishop of Canterbury, set out in the royal barge to meet the rebels. The huge threatening crowd on the river bank made them turn back. Unable to speak to the king and running short of supplies, Tyler decided to march to Lambeth where they destroyed the archbishop's records. Then they crossed London Bridge, burnt the law records in The Temple and ransacked and set fire to houses. The palace of the king's uncle, John of Gaunt, was blown up and several officials were swiftly beheaded. Besieged in the Tower, the young king watched in horror as the peasants and released prisoners ran amok.

3 It seems only a matter of time before the peasants attack the Tower.
- Spend five minutes discussing this situation in a small group, then answer these questions:
  - What should Richard do to save himself ?
  - Should he hand over his chief advisers to the rebels? Perhaps they would turn against him before he could do this?

Richard tried to address the crowd from the Tower, offering a general pardon if they went home peaceably and signing a charter to prove it. However, when two knights took the document out to read to the rebels they were shouted down and the rioting continued.

Richard then decided to send a message to the mayor to tell everyone in the city to come to the fields at Mile End next day, on pain of death, to see and hear him.

John Ball.

 What do you think Richard II would have thought of John Ball's ideas?

June 14: Richard, the mayor and a handful of lords went to Mile End. To his relief, the rebels knelt and swore loyalty. Their spokesman demanded that the 'traitors' should be handed over. Richard replied that any traitors should be tried by law; the rebels took this as an invitation to seize such criminals themselves. Richard also agreed to allow labourers to work for any wages they could get.

The murder of the Archbishop of Canterbury.

 How far does this picture drawn many years later agree with the written account on page 55?

Meanwhile the Tower had been entered by a group of peasants, apparently without any resistance by the 600 or so men at arms. They ransacked the royal chambers and found the king's advisers, including the archbishop, at prayer. Four of them were dragged outside, executed and their heads were stuck on London Bridge. The king's mother just managed to escape to another castle where Richard joined her. He signed charters confirming his promises which seemed to satisfy many of the Essex rebels who began to disperse.

---

4 The king's situation seems desperate. Yet he has made some progress by giving in to some of the rebels' demands.
- What should Richard's next move be?
- Should he deal with the Kentish peasants in the same way?
- Has he any alternative?

5 Think about the rebel leader, Wat Tyler. He is not at Mile End.
- How should he react at this point?
- Is he in a position to dictate terms to the king?
- Would it be better to try to capture the king and then make sure any promises were carried out?

June 15: The king, the mayor and a small bodyguard confronted the rebels at Smithfield. Wat Tyler rode forward, shook the king's hand and addressed him in a rude and aggressive tone. He wanted the same promises as the king had made to the Essex peasants. Tyler also demanded the abolition of all bishops except one, the confiscation of Church lands and the removal of all rights of lordship so that all men would be equal with the sole exception of the king. Richard agreed and ordered Tyler and the peasants to disperse. This willingness to grant such enormous demands probably aroused Tyler's suspicion and he noticed that the small group with the king was getting restless. An argument broke out and the mayor grew angry. He pulled Tyler from his horse and a squire stabbed the rebel leader to death as he lay on the ground.

The angry peasants closed in with a great shout but somehow the piercing voice of the young king rose above them, crying, 'Will you shoot your king? I am your captain, follow me'. His desperate action worked; perhaps it was the discipline which Tyler had developed among his army which led them to show their loyalty to the king and move away peacefully to the city walls. Before the day was over the mayor had been knighted and the head of Wat Tyler had replaced that of the Archbishop of Canterbury on London Bridge.

The End of the Revolt

While these dramatic events were taking place in London, other peasant uprisings occurred in East Anglia and Hertfordshire. However, Richard's confidence grew quickly. On June 23 he told Essex peasants 'Villeins you are and villeins you shall remain'. The rebel leaders were tried and punished; John Ball's body was cut in four in front of the king. One positive result was that poll taxes were abandoned. Although the peasants did not achieve their freedom from feudalism, the labour shortage along with other changes meant that the system of binding men and women to the lord of the manor was soon to end.

EXTENSION ACTIVITY

---

1 Why did the Peasants' Revolt fail?
- Using the information in this unit write a diary from the point of view of a rebel or a supporter of Richard.
- Try to say why the key decisions were made by Richard or Wat Tyler.
- Finish your diary by looking back at the revolt.
- Try to answer the question, 'Was Tyler certain to fail whatever he did?' Give your reasons, with regret or relief according to your point of view.

17. RICHARD III's REPUTATION

Targets

* To examine the motives of historical characters.
* To recognise gaps and bias in primary sources.

Was Richard III a good or evil king? Historians still do not agree. In this unit we will look at the evidence and try to decide.

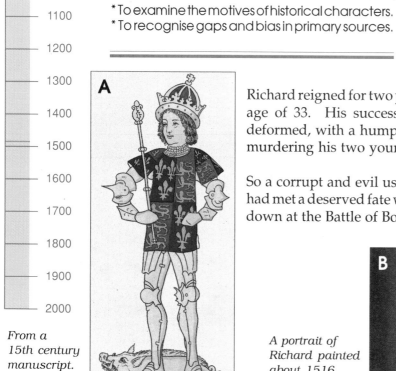

A

From a 15th century manuscript.

Richard reigned for two years, from 1483, and died in battle at the age of 33. His successors encouraged the idea that he was deformed, with a humped back, and had gained the throne by murdering his two young nephews.

So a corrupt and evil usurper (someone who seizes the throne) had met a deserved fate when Henry Tudor's bodyguard cut him down at the Battle of Bosworth Field in August 1485.

B

A portrait of Richard painted about 1516.

1483

April 9: Edward IV died suddenly. His will made his brother, Richard, protector of the kingdom until his son, Prince Edward, was old enough to rule.

April 30: Richard took the 12 year old King Edward V from the custody of his maternal uncle, Earl Rivers, and brought him from the Midlands to London for the coronation.

May 1: Queen Elizabeth Woodville, Edward V's mother, took her remaining children into sanctuary at Westminster Abbey.

June 13: Edward IV's chancellor, Lord Hastings, who was loyal to the new king, was accused by Richard of plotting.

June 16: Edward V's younger brother, Richard, joined him in the Tower of London.

June 22: Richard heard a sermon which declared Edward IV's sons were illegitimate and could not claim the throne. Therefore, Richard himself should wear the crown.

? *What sort of person does Richard seem to be in illustrations **A** and **B**?*

C

'At once, without any trial or lawful enquiry, Lord Hastings was led out on to the green beside the chapel and there, upon a block of squared timber, (without any time for confession) his head was struck off.'

The Great Chronicle of London, 1512.

D

'He and his brother were withdrawn into the inner apartments of the Tower proper, and day by day began to be seen more rarely behind the bars and windows, till at length they ceased to appear altogether.'

The Usurpation of Richard III. Domencio Mancini, 1483.

E

'Look at the events which have happened ... since the death of King Edward. Reflect how his children, already big and courageous, have been killed with impunity, and the crown has been transferred to their murderer by the favour of the people'.

Speech at Tours. Chancellor of France, January 1484.

1483

June 25: Earl Rivers was executed.

July 6: Richard III's coronation.

1484

March 1: Queen Elizabeth, widow of Edward IV, left sanctuary and gave her daughters into Richard's custody.

F

'The children of King Edward were seen shooting and playing in the garden of the Tower by sundry times ... the land was in good quiet, but after Easter (1484) there was much whispering among the people that the king had put the children of King Edward to death.'

The Great Chronicle of London. 1512.

The Tudors' View

Henry VII was happy to encourage people to believe Richard was a murderer. This helped to justify his seizure of the crown at Bosworth. In 1513 Thomas More published a book which gave details of Richard's plot to murder the princes. The idea was added to by other writers. Eventually Shakespeare's play 'Richard III' presented him as a small hunchback with a withered arm, killing anyone who got in his way.

 Who is being accused of murder by this speaker?

Edward V, based on a woodcut.

CORE ACTIVITIES

1 Look again at the information in this unit.
 ● Why did Richard seize the throne?
 ● Does the evidence suggest when he may have decided to take this step?
 ● What does this evidence suggest about the fate of the two princes in the Tower?
 ● What motives did Richard have to murder them?
 ● What facts suggest that Richard may not have killed them?

2 Now look at each source in turn.
 ● Which seem to be biased against Richard? If so, can you explain why?
 ● How useful are the illustrations as evidence about Richard's appearance and character?

EXTENSION ACTIVITY

1 Is our image of Richard mainly the result of Tudor lies?
 ● Answer this question by looking for more information.
 ● In a small group prepare a short radio programme about Richard's reign. Leave your listeners to make up their own mind about Richard but give them plenty of evidence to think about.

18. A NEW KIND OF KING?

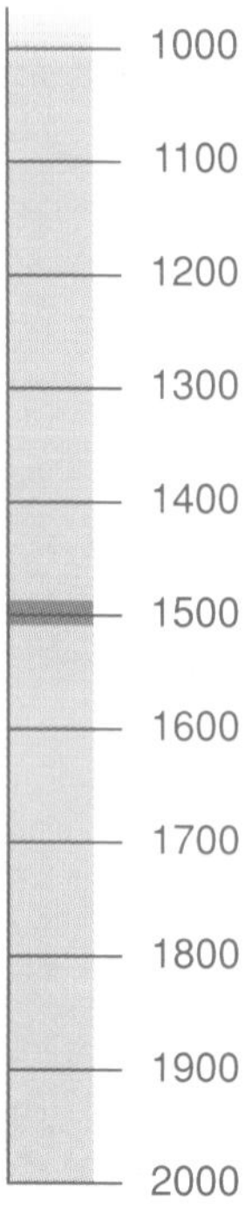

Timeline (left margin):
1000
1100
1200
1300
1400
1500
1600
1700
1800
1900
2000

Target

* To consider the achievements and new ideas of the reign of Henry VII (1485 - 1509).

1485, the year of the Battle of Bosworth Field, is often the starting point for books on 'Modern History'. For the next 118 years Tudor monarchs gave England and Wales strong central government. The Wars of the Roses, between the rival branches of the royal family, York and Lancaster, continued when two young men, Lambert Simnel and Perkin Warbeck, pretended to be the heirs of Edward IV. Henry soon defeated them. He seemed like a new type of monarch, using the law and taxes to make himself rich and free from the influence of the great barons.

Henry knew that to be strong he had to be rich. He made sure taxes and crown land rents were paid. He checked the accounts himself and kept plenty of cash in his own 'privy coffers' (private money boxes). Two debt collectors, Empson and Dudley, became very unpopular because they were so keen to make landowners pay every last penny that was due. The two unlucky men were beheaded for their efficiency! By the time he died, Henry had a fortune to leave to his son.

A leading lawyer, Francis Bacon, wrote a famous book about Henry VII in 1622. In it, he made comment about Henry's marriage to Elizabeth, daughter of Edward IV. They had four children.

A

Henry VII.

B

'It is true that all his lifetime ... he showed himself no very indulgent husband towards her, though she was beautiful, gentle, and fruitful. But his aversion towards the house of York was so predominant in him that it found place not only in his wars ... but in his chamber and bed.'

An account of Henry's marriage. Francis Bacon, 1622.

Use a dictionary to find out what indulgent and aversion mean.

C

'Henry laid down in his will that all were to be given back such possessions as had been illegally carried off to the treasury by those two most brutal extortioners.'
(Empson and Dudley)

History of England. Polydore Vergil, 1512.

Henry discouraged nobles from keeping soldiers by fining or licensing such private armies. He needed troops to call on in emergencies since he could not afford a standing army himself.

The King's Council sometimes met in a room with a night sky on the ceiling - the Star Chamber. There as a law court they offered justice to victims of riots and corruption. This checked the power of nobles who were unjust to ordinary people.

Henry used the unpaid post of Justice of the Peace to give his own chosen servants responsibility for local government. The Council made sure they did as the king, not a local lord, wished.

Like Edward IV, Henry used churchmen as leading advisers. He also followed Edward's example in raising money from free gifts called benevolences. Archbishop Morton stayed at rich houses. If the owners did not show him hospitality, then they must be misers and could afford to give money to the king. If they appeared lavish, they had plenty of cash to spare for Henry. This 'tails I win, heads you lose' method was called Morton's Fork.

Margaret Beaufort, Henry's mother.

Henry himself was not a miser. He spent lavishly on royal ceremonies, banquets, jousts and Church festivals. He also built a new palace at Richmond and had a menagerie of rare animals.

CORE ACTIVITIES

1 Think about Henry's achievements.
  ● Draw a table like the one below.

NOBLES	YORKISTS	MONEY	LAW
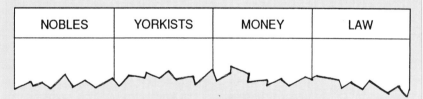			

  ● Note down at least three different facts in each column.
  ● Compare and discuss your completed list with a partner.
  ● Try to agree what was the most important success of Henry in each column.
  ● What evidence can you find to indicate that Henry was following the example of Edward IV?

2 Look at the pictures of Henry and his mother.
  ● How would you sum up the sort of people they seem to have been from this evidence?

3 Think about the rest of the evidence on these pages.
  ● What else can you say about Henry's character?

EXTENSION ACTIVITY

1 You have just heard the news of Henry's death in 1509.
  ● Working with a friend, use the evidence on these pages and your own conclusions to prepare a role-play. One of you is very sorry because you thought the king was kind and brought peace to the land. The other, a rich person who secretly still supports the Yorkists, is not afraid to express his anger over some of Henry's activities.
  ● Are you likely to agree or will there be an argument?
  ● When you have jotted down the main points for your discussion, record it on tape.

19. OUT OF THE MIDDLE AGES

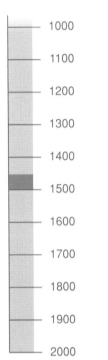

1000
1100
1200
1300
1400
1500
1600
1700
1800
1900
2000

Targets

* To investigate the changes which were taking place in the 15th century.
* To identify points of similarity and difference between England in 1066 and 1500.

You could take any span of 50 years and say it was a time of change. However, there are periods when things seem to change more quickly and soon the world seems to be a very different place.

Historians have called the century between 1450 and 1550 the period of Renaissance or 'rebirth' in Western Europe. In England the start of the Tudor period in 1485 has been a convenient point to date the end of the medieval period and the start of the modern age. What changes may have marked this transition from medieval to modern times? We will look at several in this unit; let us start with time itself.

Between 1350-90, the first public clocks appeared in churches. They only had an hour hand. The minute hand was added c.1400. Soon the first portable clocks were invented.

 Why do you think the exact time of day was less important to most people in the Middle Ages than nowadays?

By 1480-1500, Portuguese and Spanish explorers reached America, southern Africa and India. Treasure, slaves and later new crops such as sugar, tobacco and cotton brought immense wealth to Europe in the next 400 years.

 How do you think these voyages might have affected people living in Europe?

Between 1492-1600, 750 000 lbs of gold reached Spain from South America. The results of this included greater use of cash instead of payment in kind. Trade grew and some merchants became bankers , especially in Italy.

 Why do you think the imports of gold and silver lead to an increase in the supply of coins?

Printers at work.

 How do you think information and knowledge spread before the invention of the printing press?

The first printing office in Europe was set up by Johann Gutenberg, in 1448, at Mainz in Germany. The Chinese had discovered how to make paper and block printing. Movable metal type speeded up the process and by 1500, ten million books had been produced. These included many religious and ancient works as well as 'grammars' which helped large numbers of children learn to read.

In 1494, the invasion of Italy by the French king, Charles VIII, showed how gunpowder had changed warfare. His bronze field artillery destroyed castle walls with ease. Soon infantry armed with muskets added to the firepower. Success in war became much more expensive, allowing governments rather than local lords to keep control by force.

Noble ladies in a carriage.

Around 1485 the first coaches appeared in towns, otherwise land travel did not change. Roads were frequently too muddy to use in winter. Messages were carried by horsemen up to 100 miles in a day.

The Renaissance was the result of looking back to the great civilisations of Greece and Rome. Their ideas, books, art and architecture inspired the rich and educated throughout Western Europe.

Italy, the country where these ancient examples were best preserved, was the place to visit. This heritage influenced artists like Michelangelo and Leonardo da Vinci who produced drawings, paintings and sculpture which remain the greatest treasures of Europe today.

The countryside was still dominated by castles but the next century saw nobles becoming more interested in building manor houses than draughty fortresses.

Most villages still had their open fields but increasingly these were disappearing in favour of sheep runs. Some villages had even been destroyed to make way for these 'enclosures'. For many people the pace and routine of life was not so different from that of their ancestors in 1066. The Church was still the centre of village life: the seasons still governed people's activities and news still travelled slowly to the isolated communities along the muddy rutted trackways of the kingdom.

Of course it is easy to find ways in which very little was changing in this period. In England the king still ruled with the help and advice of his barons and leading churchmen. In battle he still led an army which was raised from knights and archers who were employed by their local lord.

A weak king still brought the risk of civil war. Henry VII's reign brought to an end a long period of fighting between groups of noblemen. However, he used taxation and his law courts to control anyone who ignored royal authority.

By 1500 the population was about 3 million - twice as many as in 1066 but much fewer than the 4.75 million people alive on the eve of the Black Death. London was at least four times bigger than in 1066. The growth of wool and cloth exports in particular made it a thriving market and port as well as the centre of government.

A drawing by Leonardo da Vinci (1452-1519) of the Virgin and Child with two saints.

In the few other towns, merchants were growing prosperous and building larger houses. These were still timber framed with thatched roofs, but more spacious and comfortable.

A merchant's town house, preserved at Bromsgrove.

CORE ACTIVITIES

1 Think about the changes you have read about.
 ● Write a sentence about the results of each change in this period.
 ● Which changes would have been the most important in the lives of:
  - townspeople
  - villagers
  - monks
  - merchants

2 Read this section again.
 ● What examples can you find of continuity rather than change?
 ● Why do you think historians see 1500 as the end of an era?
 ● Why did people living in the 19th century call this era 'The Middle Ages'?
  (*CLUE TO SUCCESS*: Look at a timeline of British or European history from the time of Jesus Christ to the present day*)*

EXTENSION ACTIVITY

1 Use this book and any other material available to you.
 ● Prepare a short presentation to answer one of the following questions.
  - How did medieval monarchs control the nobles, peasants and the Church?
  - What power and influence did the Church have on medieval England and Wales?
  - What changes made life better for villagers and townsfolk between 1066 and 1500?
  - What kinds of evidence have survived from the Middle Ages? Give examples to show which are the most useful and reliable.
  (*CLUE TO SUCCESS*: You may wish to work in small groups. Try role-play for different points of view, displays of cuttings, postcards and drawings and possibly video or audio tapes to make your presentation vivid and enjoyable!*)*

INDEX